The Contentment Dilemma

Examining Life's Mysteries and Purposes

Marcus Hurst

Unless otherwise indicated, all Scriptures references are from the Holy Bible, English Standard Version®. Copyright © 2001 by Crossway, a publishing ministry of Good News Publishers.

Parentheses in quotations indicate the author's emphasis.

Cover design by Jude Mag-asin

Printed in the United States of America.

ISBN: 979-8-88759-691-4 - paperback

ISBN: 979-8-88759-692-1 - ebook

ISBN: 979-8-88759-956-4 - hardcover

Table of Contents

The Contentment Dilemma

Acknowledgments

God is the sole reason for this book. He coached me through
the entire process and encouraged me when I came to
hard places. I worked closely with Him on developing
the needed points.

I want to acknowledge the priceless help of the many
friends, relatives, ministers, and author associates who
proofread the manuscript and offered suggestions. My
parents and brothers sufficiently handed out opinions
upon request.

I also want to acknowledge professionals I got in
contact with through reedsy.com and
selfpublishing.com, who helped fine-tune this book and
get me through the daunting publication process:

- Eric Muhr – reedsy.com (Developmental editor)
- Jordyn Feyen – selfpublishing.com (Book Production Coordinator)
- Mike Doane – reedsy.com (Publishing advisor)
- Scott Allen – selfpublishing.com (Coach)
- Sky Rodio Nuttall – selfpublishing.com (Editor)

Introducing The Contentment Dilemma

*Discouragement is dissatisfaction with the
past, distaste for the present, and dismay
about the future.[1] – William Ward*

Is human life nothing more than working hard and trying to have fun without getting into too much trouble? Can anything bring us lasting encouragement and fulfillment during our few years of existence?

King Solomon was known throughout the ancient world for his exceptional wealth and wisdom. Yet, even he had questions regarding life's purpose. Solomon recorded a detailed description of his unfruitful search for contentment in Ecclesiastes 2. After he had all this wealth and fame, he wrote, "Then I considered all that my hands had done and the toil I had expended in doing it, and behold, all was vanity and a striving after wind, and there was nothing to be gained under the sun" (Ecclesiastes 2:11).

Many people focus on acquiring wealth and the approval of friends, for they believe these pursuits will bring them greater happiness. But like Solomon, if they get the prosperity and acceptance they desire, do these bring the expected contentment?

Ask celebrities if their wealth and fame give them a satisfied mind, and you will find that these conditions do not bring lasting satisfaction. Although wealth and popularity produce brief enjoyment at best, are these folks not often craving more, and rarely inclined just to relax and be content?

I once came across the following statement that sums up Solomon's experience: "Those who demand that their world conforms to their desires are among the most insecure and dependent folks."[2]

Insecurity and life's uncertainties plague the wealthy just as it does other people. Though insurance is available for many unexpected inconveniences, does it bring the peace of mind its users anticipate?

What, then, will bring us the sense of security we so desire? How can we identify a remedy to aid us in this fulfillment dilemma?

Ivan Weaver well described the contentment of which I speak when he wrote, "Contentment is not an emotional experience, but rather a deep-seated, calm serenity that is absent of the pressure of our peers and the expectations of social norms."[3]

My heart goes out to the many individuals searching for peace of mind, for I have also made that painful journey.

* * * * *

I welcome you to accompany me, my friend, as we tackle these questions and look at some answers that have helped me secure inner peace. I hope you can also find these explanations reliable and the solutions rewarding.

I attempt to present the truth in its purest form. As we explore these topics, do not hesitate to disagree with me if necessary. Though I have tried to do my research, my understanding may be more limited than I realize.

This book touches briefly on various topics. If you desire more details, I invite you to do your own research. Throughout these chapters, I mention books that cover specific subjects more thoroughly.

I also want to clarify that I cannot endorse everything written and spoken by the quoted writers. Although they make some remarkable points, I do not support everything these authors believe.

You will find a question in a text box, when a question and answer on the subject are in the Q&A section at the back.

Multitudes in this great valley's division,
Seeking to know what is truth and is light;
Seeking to make that great final decision,
Wanting to know the great answers of life.[4]
– John Esh

The Contentment Dilemma

1. The Value of Truth

Sometimes people don't want to hear the
truth because they don't want their illusions
destroyed.[5] – Friedrich Nietzsche

The creep of post-truth is seen in how we gather
information about the world to conform to what we want
to be true, not to what actually is true.[6] – Abdu Murray

The truth will set you free. (John 8:32)

Harold likes to drive his car, but the route he needs
to take goes through a congested urban area with many
traffic lights, and he cannot drive as fast as he wants.

However, that won't be a problem on his way home
tonight because Harold thought of a solution. He will
set the cruise control at 55 miles per hour, and if a
vehicle is in front of him, he'll just believe it is not there.
And if he comes to a red light, he'll just believe it is
green, so he should arrive home in record time...

Yes, we agree it would be foolish to set the cruise
control at 55 mph through a congested area and assume
it will work out. But is it not common practice to
fabricate and support any lie we imagine will make us
feel better?

We will not escape the truth as we drive down the

road, and nor will we, in the end, evade any other truths in life.

Hasn't avoiding the truth always been a cruel and disappointing road to travel?

I think we can agree that it is essential to maintain an open mind to the truth and bravely pursue it. Is anything as secure as confidently standing on the solid ground of certainty? And is anything as repulsive as struggling through swamps of falsehood and error?

If we hold conflicting ideas, we cannot all be correct, even if we convince ourselves we are right. Considering the countless contradicting opinions that abound, we can note that many people who are sure they are right are mistaken. In reality, it could be we who are wrong.

One might wonder, if we can know the truth about life, why there are so many contradicting opinions.

Are diverse views not often the result of people, especially those who are highly influential, refusing to accept ideas that contradict what they want to think? These folks are not afraid to assert their opinion as fact, regardless of reality. This bias leaves them and those they influence with a dreadfully distorted perspective of the issue. Will we find the truth if our preferences are more important to us than factual evidence?

I also fight the tendency to base my conclusions on my biased opinions. I must repeatedly remind myself that accepting reality will be far more rewarding than only believing what I want to think.

How about you? Are you willing to discredit desired opinions for the sake of truth?

Do we admit that our reasoning may be far more incorrect than we would like to think?

As it has been said, "There are none who are as deaf as those who do not want to hear."[7] Blaise Pascal also noted, "Truth is so obscure in these times, and falsehood so established, that unless we love the truth, we cannot know it."[8]

What we want to believe can easily influence our reasoning; thus, if we are unwilling to accept the truth at all costs, we likely do not know the truth.

Taking a thorough and honest look at a view that does not interest us is certainly challenging. Jonathan Swift wrote, "Reasoning itself is true and just, but the reasoning of every man is weak and wavering, perpetually swayed and turned by his interest, his passions, and his vices."[9] No wonder folks are confused about reality when it is so common to allow our preferences to distort our view of the truth.

In *Time for Truth*, Os Guinness wrote, "Truth is true even if nobody believes it, and falsehood is false even if everybody believes it. That is why truth does not yield to opinion, fashion, numbers, office, or sincerity—it is simply true, and that is the end of it. ... In this modern age, more and more people are all surface, skills, and résumé—and no character. ... By the end of the 20th century, it was widely accepted that old notions, such as 'true self,' had gone the way of common-sense real-ity."[10]

In his blog, Steve Simms shared, "The exaltation of desire is leading our culture to sacrifice truth, reason, and conscience. It takes courage to be awakened enough to search for truth when the truth doesn't contain what we desire."[11]

Personally, I have clamored after my desires and

tasted the discontent that accompanies those who ignore the truth. At other times, I have pursued truth without reserve and enjoyed the resulting blessing of security and assurance of locating an accurate explanation. Oh, that I would never step away from the truth again. But I still get caught up in myself at times, and once again enter that loathsome, despondent condition that accompanies such action.

Emotions can also be a hindrance when searching for truth. Our emotions are unstable and inconsistent. For example, if Jim gets angry at his dog, Rover, and decides it would be nice to put Rover to sleep forever, should Jim kill his dog because his emotions tell him it would make him feel better?

Part of the reason we are confused is that we believe and act based on how we feel about the situation. For example, because Jane and her husband Jake's emotions differ on some issues, they decide to get a divorce.

No matter how real they are, our emotions will never change reality. However, that does not mean we cannot trust our sense of affection towards our friends. Although we cannot trust our feelings as a rule, we still need to consider them.

Some people may confidently retain their viewpoints, not out of self-confidence or emotion, but they have never considered that they might be mistaken. Many people believe what their peers say, or what they have always thought, without questioning the credibility of the information.

Also, it is the general environment many folks are in that trains them to fend for themselves and avoid inconvenient truths.

Everybody makes mistakes, and it takes courage to admit our errors and pursue correct alternatives. For myself, many times, when I was sure my view was correct, someone showed me I was wrong after all. For such reasons, it is best to recognize that we could be incorrect, even when we think we have things figured out.

Our craving for fulfillment, as well as all other problems in humanity, have a complete and accessible solution, and avoiding that remedy will only bring us despair. To find peace, we must accept reality and respond accordingly.

There are many contradicting views to be accepted by any who will listen. The only sure method of locating truth is to dedicate ourselves to reality, no matter how revolting and challenging it may appear.

Many people find the truth intimidating, and I admit it is not for cowards. However, although accepting the facts is difficult, it is a vital step we must take on our journey toward locating the fulfillment we crave.

I assure you, my friend, that having no bias to defend will be worth every effort. Avoiding truth will never bring us the level of comfort we seek—it will always make us miserable in the end.

I have discovered that unbiasedly standing for truth leads to the contentment the world desires, which is available to everyone. But yes, submitting to the truth's authority can be a significant challenge.

We know that many people avoid inconvenient truths as much as possible, and many are dissatisfied. Thus, is it not likely that the solution to our plight appears scary at a glance, thereby causing folks to avoid the very thing they desire?

In *Mere Christianity*, C. S. Lewis suggests, "Comfort is the one thing you cannot get by looking for it. If you look for truth, you may find comfort in the end: if you look for comfort you will not get either comfort or truth, only soft soap and wishful thinking, to begin with, and in the end, despair."[12]

We must brave up and face our fears. Seeking relief from our problems through such avenues as energy drinks, smoking, doing drugs, or hiding any negative truth about ourselves from others, will not help us here.

(To read more on finding truth in this 21st century, check out Abdu Murray's book *Saving Truth*.)

The World's Deadliest Disaster —The Me-Infection Pandemic

By defending the ideas they want to support and ignoring the ones they would rather not find, many people disregard inconvenient facts in favor of preferred opinions. Charles Caleb Colton noted, "Men have discovered it is far more convenient to adulterate the truth than to refine themselves."[13]

Multitudes seek and indulge in wealth, fame, thrill, and immorality, while taking minimal consideration for the people around them as they pursue what they imagine will make them happy. (We will call these people me-folks because of their self-centered attitude, and we will call this attitude the me-infection.) This restless sensation of self-love has been moving through humanity for thousands of years. Indeed, have we not all struggled with the me-infection?

Over the centuries, billions have suffered severe emotional and physical injury as me-folks brush past them in their rampant pursuit of personal desires.

Some research revealed that over a third of the sixty million annual human deaths may result from selfishness, with millions more suffering me-infection-related agony.

Below are some statistics, based on research I did in 2022, on the global self-centered-related deaths and suffering that we experience each year. Although these cases are not all a direct product of the me-infection, these numbers help illustrate how prevalent and destructive greed is.

- There are nine million starvations, and eight hundred million people are undernourished,[14] which is 11% of the world's population.
- One billion children suffer violence.[15]
- About seven hundred thirty-six million women experience physical or sexual violence.[16]
- There are about seventy-three million induced abortions.[17]
- There are around five hundred sixty thousand deaths from conflict and murder,[18] not to mention conflict-related suffering.
- About five hundred thousand deaths are from drug use.[19]
- There are about three million alcohol-related deaths.[20]
- About 45% of all marriages end in divorce.[21]

Me-infection related Suffering Compared to the Population of Three Major Regions

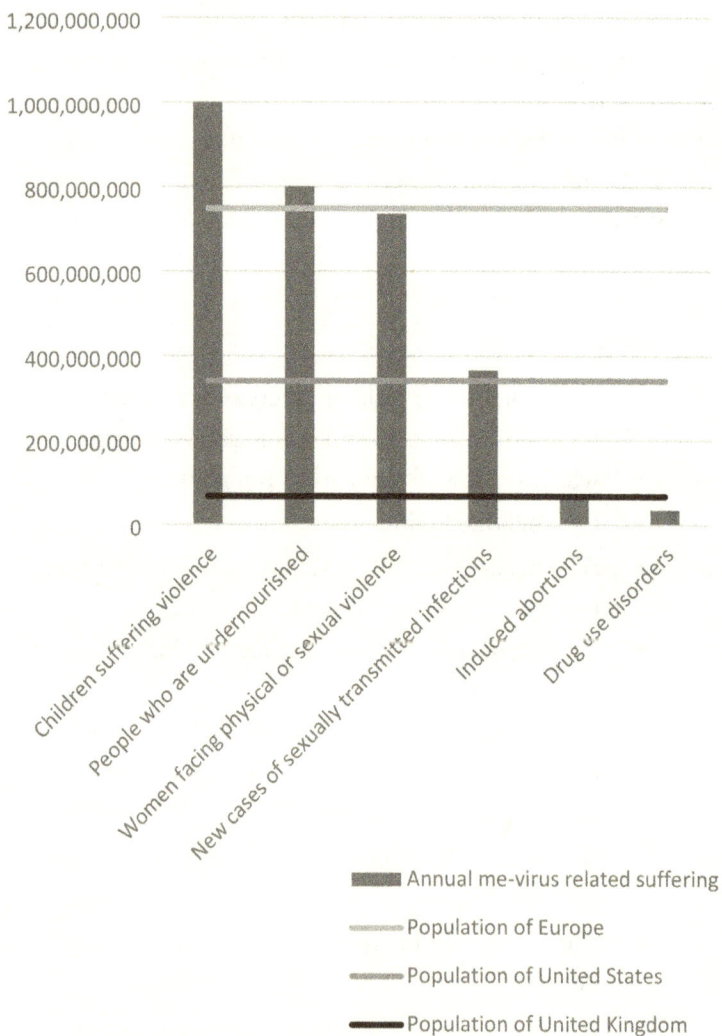

▬	Annual me-virus related suffering
▬	Population of Europe
▬	Population of United States
▬	Population of United Kingdom

X-axis categories:
- Children suffering violence
- People who are undernourished
- Women facing physical or sexual violence
- New cases of sexually transmitted infections
- Induced abortions
- Drug use disorders

Y-axis values: 0, 200,000,000, 400,000,000, 600,000,000, 800,000,000, 1,000,000,000, 1,200,000,000

Me-infection related Deaths Compared to the Population of Three American Cities

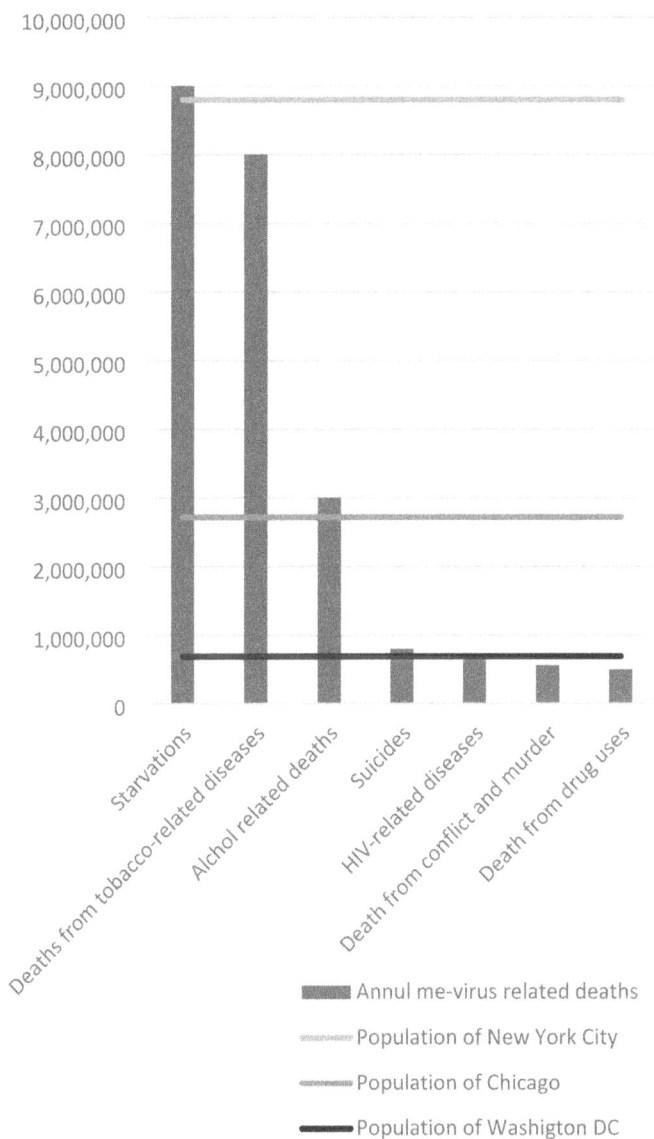

Legend:
- Annul me-virus related deaths
- Population of New York City
- Population of Chicago
- Population of Washigton DC

Categories: Starvations, Deaths from tobacco-related diseases, Alchol related deaths, Suicides, HIV-related diseases, Death from conflict and murder, Death from drug uses

Y-axis values: 0, 1,000,000, 2,000,000, 3,000,000, 4,000,000, 5,000,000, 6,000,000, 7,000,000, 8,000,000, 9,000,000, 10,000,000

Other annual rates of deaths and suffering, of which the connection to selfishness may be more controversial, include:

- Eight million deaths occur from tobacco-related diseases.
- 1.2 million are from second-hand smoke.[22]
- Eight hundred thousand suicides.[23]
- About three hundred sixty-five million new cases of sexually transmitted infections (That is one million new cases each day.)[24] and six hundred fifty thousand deaths from HIV-related diseases.[25]
- Over thirty-five million people suffer from drug use disorders.

Thus, we find ourselves in the middle of a global and persistent me-infection pandemic.

The more one thinks about it, the more one will realize the seriousness and urgency of this frightful situation.

Upon consideration, can you think of any intentional crime or heated dispute that did not likely result from uncontrolled pride? Is this circumstance not the root cause of all political unrest, social division, family contention, dishonesty, and poverty? This makes the me-infection the most widespread and destructive epidemic in history.

Is this self-centered appetite not part of our genetic makeup? But that fact does not mean we cannot overcome it. With God's help, we can rise above any less-than-ideal mindset or attitude.

Unlike medical infections, the me-infection is a

choice. If we are selfish, we choose to have the me-infection and are the only person responsible for it and the damage it does to other people.

The me-infection, along with every attitude and action it leads to, is a sin and will restrain us from being in God's will and favor until repented of. Every act of selfishness drives us farther away from the contentment we crave. There is nothing like not eventually regretting one's selfish attitude.

Let me share a story a friend told me, which illustrates the grandeur of communities that live for the well-being of others.

My friend told how his father's food processing facility burned down, and with the help of 90 people who donated time and materials to help, they rebuilt the structure in three days.

Also, in three days his father had the funds from the insurance company, which covered half the rebuilding expenses, even when they added various improvements from what had been there.

He also shared that they are not sure what started the fire, and there is no guarantee it wasn't arson. But the community trusted that his father didn't burn it down himself to collect insurance and get a good deal on a fresh facility.

He said that experience really opened his eyes to the power and blessing of an honest reputation and a loving and trusting community.

The Evasion of Inconvenient Truths

Me-folks have encountered some obstacles in only

acknowledging what they want to think. One of these has been their conscience. When they do the things they want, something in their head may advise them it is not a good act to perform.

But my folks are sure if they want it, it must be good to get. They soon find that if they ignore their conscience and tell themselves it does not matter, that voice will diminish and presently expire.

Logic has also become an interference for many; however, me-folks have found their conscience remedy also works on reason. If they refuse to consider logic and instead focus on what they want to think, they can believe it anyhow. Openly mocking the opinions they do not wish to acknowledge has also helped these people feel better about accepting illogical views. The me-infection can lead to an attitude Abdu Murray mentioned, when he wrote:

> Confusion is embraced as a virtue and clarity shunned as a sin.
>
> But as our culture has embraced confusion and shunned clarity, have we found ourselves to be better off? The divisiveness of our rhetoric is corrosive. Those who disagree with us are "them." Facts often seem to be a problem to get around instead of the useful tools they once were. And if someone takes a stand we disagree with on a particular issue, we label them in the most uncharitable way possible, never mind whether they may have a point.[26]

Another issue that me-folks have run into is the

moral code. Throughout the ages, many governments and cultures endorsed laws of moral correctness that God had introduced, but many people resist these moral laws.

When we set a goal, anything that hinders us from reaching that goal becomes an unwanted obstacle. Will it not be natural to try working around that obstacle so we can attain our goal?

Having made their personal desires their goal, me-folks see the idea of an all-powerful super-being telling them how to live as a significant obstacle. As Steve Simms mentioned, "To be comfortable with sin requires an ongoing effort to be unaware of God."[27] It has consequently become the ambition of millions to avoid and minimize God.

The passionate craving for no moral restraint has undermined folk's respect for the truth, leading to the invention of naturalism. This worldview requires no supernatural authority, and thus, no moral code.

In brief, naturalism states that a piece of matter exploded billions of years ago. This "Big Bang" initiated a chain of events that, over billions of years, resulted in the universe we know today. According to this theory, all life evolved from a single living organism that developed from non-living matter.

Many me-folks find it terrifying to think someone knows everything about them. Why believe in this "big boss" when it is much handier to disregard Him, live as we please, and consider ourselves accountable to nobody? What incredible appeal! Is it no wonder naturalism has enthusiastic support and is now taught as a fact of science? As a result, many cultures have slackened their stand on moral issues, giving me-folks more liberty to do what they want.

In our modern age, does one not need humility to grasp the ins and outs of submitting to the creation story and still believe it? And we know humility is a thing many people intentionally avoid.

Jesus says, "The light has come into the world, and people loved the darkness rather than the light because their works were evil. For everyone who does wicked things hates the light and does not come to the light, lest his works should be exposed" (John 3:19–20).

Referring to God, Apostle Paul stated, "For his invisible attributes, namely, his eternal power and divine nature, have been clearly perceived, since the creation of the world, in the things that have been made. So they are without excuse. For although they knew God, they did not honor him as God or give thanks to him, but they became futile in their thinking, and their foolish hearts were darkened. Claiming to be wise, they became fools" (Romans 1:20–22).

Steve Simms shared about this situation: "Every time you deny the truth, you chain your free will to a lie. … When your will is enslaved by deception, desire, addiction, or obsession, you've given up your freedom to choose your behaviors."[28]

* * * * *

Apostle Paul prophesied the widespread pursuit of one's personal desires nearly two thousand years ago when he wrote, "But understand this, that in the last days there will come times of difficulty. For people will be lovers of self, lovers of money, proud, arrogant, abusive, disobedient to their parents, ungrateful, unholy, heartless, unappeasable, slanderous, without self-control … always learning and never able to arrive at a knowledge of the truth" (2 Timothy 3:1–4, 7). Notice that Paul suggests the difficulty we experience results from our self-centeredness.

Though billions of people have enthusiastically rejected the facts, they have never changed. All liars will someday regret denying the truth, though they may not admit it in this life. If we are alive and have the mental capacity, it is not too late to pursue and embrace reality.

The Humble Cure

This me-infection pandemic is not a disease to be treated by medication, but with healthy choices and self-denial.

We will do well to prioritize the truth and the well-being of others ahead of our personal desires. Our lives are not all about ourselves and what we can get from them. Truthfully, those who live like that were the case are the miserable ones. Living for self will always lead us to a wretched existence.

A humble and selfless attitude is an essential component in any fact-locating endeavor. And let me clarify that being humble does not mean you need to walk around with gloomy expressions; neither does it include downgrading yourself or considering yourself a nobody.

After all, what is more powerful, peaceful, and awe-inspiring than true heartfelt humility?

Yes, humility appears weak, while pride looks

powerful. But consider which will produce fulfillment quicker: The power of pride in telling and believing lies and insulting anyone who dares to challenge our preferences, or the power and peace of humility when we pursue truth without compromise and calmly discuss differences until we can reach an agreement?

Humility unlocks the graceful maneuvers of self-control, while pride binds it with heavy chains and has folks fly off the handle instead. How awe-inspiring to hear, "I'm sorry, I was mistaken about that. You are right, after all."

We have analyzed life's contentment dilemma and considered the importance of accepting the facts, even when they are distasteful. Let us now, my friend, with courage and humility, set out to defend the truth and uncover any hidden nuggets of reality.

> The more I strain to love myself
> The more I'm caught in a heavy chain.
> Instead of helping me gain inner peace,
> It increases my pain.[29]
>
> — Steve Simms

> Even today men are faced with hard choices,
> Offered the truth, but not willing to turn;
> Challenged from right by the multitude's voices,
> Fighting the warfare of truth to discern.[30]
>
> — John Esh

2. Acknowledging Spiritual Reality

It's the person who wants to know God that God
reveals himself to. And if a person doesn't want to
know God—well, God has created the world and
the human mind in such a way that he doesn't have
to... God ordained that people should be governed
in the end by what they want.[31] – Dallas Willard

I want to start this chapter by acknowledging the
existence of two supernatural authorities: God [the
original and unrestricted] and Satan [the devil]. After
summarizing God and Satan's functionalities, I will
share a few personal testimonies of their existence.
Then, in the following chapters, we shall consider
further details concerning these beings.

* * * * *

God is the mastermind behind the universe and
every form of life, and He has supreme power over His
creation. Being inherently good, God did not create
moral corruption. However, He made every other detail
of our world and established scientific laws to govern it.

In earthly terms, God put a lot of thought into His
work. Every feature of His creation has a specific
purpose, and He truly cares about each detail. God put

special effort into making us humans, and He especially loves and cares for His signature humanity.

Question 1: Does God really care about these tiny humans dwelling on one of the billions of planets He created?

God is interested in human lives and cherishes each of us. No sin, history, or race can lessen God's love for one person over another. Furthermore, God desires to associate with us personally. He sees great potential in each of us. In fact, He would not have made us if He did not have a plan for us.

As gasoline engines run best on gasoline, God has designed us to function best when we maintain a close connection with Him and dedicate ourselves to His will (Psalms 34:4–10). Jesus says, "If you abide in my word, you are truly my disciples, and you will know the truth, and the truth will set you free" (John 8:31–32).

An intimate relationship with God is the only satisfying answer to the continuing sense of fulfillment and security that humanity craves. He has placed this restless desire deep within us that we might diligently seek a solution until we find it.

Out of profound love for us, God permitted men to torture and crucify His son, Jesus Christ, to take the place of the deserved punishment of all other persons. "For one will scarcely die for a righteous person though perhaps for a good person one would dare even to die. But God shows his love for us in that while we were still sinners, Christ died for us" (Romans 5:7–8).

Because of His unconditional love for us, God is exceptionally patient and is quick to forgive any lamented offense upon a humble request (Psalms 86:5

and 1 John 1:9).

Instead of operating us like puppets, God gave us the independence to make our own decisions, and He has chosen never to force His will upon us. God respects our choices and allows us to avoid

Question 2: What may have been God's motive to give us choice?

Him if we choose. Instead of openly punishing us as soon as we transgress, He has given us the independence to believe what we want to think and live how we choose to live.

✳ ✳ ✳ ✳ ✳

On the other hand, Satan is the source of confusion, hatred, and all moral corruption (James 3:14-16). He craves to distress and destroy all humanity.

Upon getting a grip on his victims, Satan will distort their reasoning and train them to accept his lies, avoid the truth, and become his faithful assistants (John 8:42–44). Satan's grip on his victims includes seeing that making a change for God and right living is vigorously spine-chilling and inconvenient.

Imagine what damage an epidemic could do if we believed it did not exist, and consider what Satan can accomplish in a society that denies his reality.

Satan desperately does not want us to analyze our lives and conclude that we should pursue God's will. Have we not all experienced his tactics as he endeavors to discourage us and distract us from the truth? However, God does not mind if we

Question 3: If God and Satan are both in the universe, how is God not contaminated by the devil?

offend Satan; actually, He instructs us to resist him (James 4:7). You will never regret pushing past the devil and pursuing God's peace and righteousness.

* * * * *

Jesus tells his followers, "If you love me, you will keep my commandments. And I will ask the Father, and he will give you another Helper, to be with you forever, even the Spirit of truth, whom the world cannot receive, because it neither sees him nor knows him. You know him, for he dwells with you and will be in you." (John 14:15-17).

Here, Jesus promised to give his people a helper, whom he calls the Spirit of Truth. He suggests that the people who do not keep his commandments cannot know the truth, for Satan had blinded them to it. The truth sometimes appears foolish to unbelievers, for they cannot fully comprehend its benefits until they yield to God and gain freedom from satanic deception.

Personal Testimony of God's Existence

I have asked myself, "What is the chance God does not exist?"

After seriously considering that question, I have concluded there is no chance.

After I surrendered my life to God's will and asked Him to forgive my trespasses against Him, the joy and security that immediately enveloped my being were beyond description. For the first time, I felt entirely satisfied.

Even now, I feel insecure and find myself groping

for peace when I lose focus and again pursue my sensual ambitions. But I experience profound inner serenity when I surrender my life to God and pursue His will.

I have trusted God and the Bible for many years, and they have not let me down; neither can I adequately describe feeling guilt-free and assured of being fully in God's will. I have concluded that this is the fulfillment humanity craves to secure and pursues in some strange ways.

By myself, this book would not have materialized. It was God who got after me to write this work and patiently walked me through the countless hours of its creation and publication.

Question 4: People from other belief systems associate with their gods and can feel at peace. How can you be sure your relationship with God is real while theirs is counterfeit?

Instead of pursuing a college education, I have relied on God to teach me what I need to know. Sometimes His lessons are painful and scary, but relying on God has been worth it. He never failed me and always gives me what it takes to get my "homework" done.

Here is an example of my education through life's experiences: When I was nineteen, I had pride and excessive self-confidence as I started my first job. God fed me quite a bit of humble pie as He tried to get my attention and show me my error. I was not mature enough to handle the job's required responsibilities. Eight months into it, God concluded that intense "training session" by having me fired. The lessons I learned through that adventure proved invaluable to me. However, I had to learn some of them again because I forgot.

Six years later, I was asked to take a similar job. I did

Question 5: Can you explain more about how you are sure it is God speaking to you?

not want the position and thought I had a good reason to turn it down, but to my dismay, God made it clear that I should take the job. I accepted the position, which proved to be another of life's invaluable experiences.

That adventure turned out much better. I am glad I did it, for looking back it is clear that it has dramatically influenced my life for the better.

Testimony of Satan's Existence

I have ample evidence that Satan despises righteousness. He places persistent, immoral thoughts in my mind, hoping I dwell on them and let them lure me away from my relationship with God. Thankfully, God faithfully responds to my cries for deliverance, and when I rebuke Satan and seek God's presence these temptations retreat.

When I served at Red Rock Refuge [a counseling facility for teenage boys], I found the residents behaved much better when I asked God to suppress Satan's influence.

Following is an account of God delivering me from Satan's presence.

> **August 12th, 2021** – Early this morning, I was restless and could not sleep. When I tried to pray, it felt like there was a kink in the hose, so to speak. My

thoughts refused to focus, and God seemed distant and out of reach.

I finally realized God was too far away, which meant Satan was too close. So I asked God to remove Satan's presence as far away as the east is from the west and replace it with His presence. I promptly started feeling better and briefly waited as the transaction completed and I could fully sense God's presence and peace.

My gratitude was beyond words. I felt so unworthy of God's immediate response to my dilemma.

I learned an important lesson: Whenever I feel restless and not in God's presence, the problem is Satan's presence, and you just read the solution.

I was still hot and couldn't sleep, but the "kink in the hose" was gone; my thoughts were relaxed and concentrated, and I felt at peace.

Around 3:30, I prayed for a deep, relaxed rest and soon fell asleep. When my alarm went off at 5:40, I felt I was waking from an especially deep sleep.

I still encounter the appalling awareness of Satan's presence at times, but it never lasts long.

> I have found the joy no tongue can tell,
> How its waves of glory roll!
> It is like a great o'er flowing well,
> Springing up within my soul.[32]
> – B. E. Warren

The Contentment Dilemma

3. God, the Only Source

Other people have a concept of God so fundamentally
false that it would be better for them to doubt than to
remain devout. The more devout they are, the uglier their
faith will become since it is based on a lie. Doubt in such
a case is not only highly understandable, it is even a mark
of spiritual and intellectual sensitivity to error, for their
picture is not of God but an idol.[33] – Os Guinness

Now, let us examine God's functionality.

Because God is not a physical being, He is not
bound by space. (In other words, He is no particular
size.) God also is not subject to time as we are; thus, He
simultaneously and thoroughly keeps track of
everything that happens. Nothing escapes His
attention. He knows
our needs, passions,
addictions, and even
our thoughts. Ulti-
mately, God under-
stands us far better
than we know our-
selves.

**Question 6: How can we
effectively choose what we
will do if God already
knows the future? And why
did God create humans if
He knew they were going
to be so corrupt?**

Communicating with God

When God created Earth, He appointed man as stewards over its extent. We are the only creatures with a nonphysical soul, which enables us to communicate with God and Satan.

If we process messages for God to hear, whether spoken or merely thought, He will understand. In return, God will place thoughts and emotions into our minds; thus, we can converse. Indeed, one priceless detail about associating with God is that He will never misunderstand us.

When God "speaks" to us, the experience can be distinct and incredibly real, to the extent that even skeptics may have no doubt of its source.

In the Bible, God promises to be there for us and never let us down. He is always available to hear us out and help us through life's problems. I know, it frequently appears like God has blown these promises, but I find this notion to merely be an illusion. It is a story Satan is parading in front of us in hopes that we will stop trusting God.

Only after we connect with God can He help us discern truth from error in the various complex subjects of life. Jesus says, "If you love me, you will keep my commandments. And I will ask the Father, and he will give you another Helper, to be with you forever, even the Spirit of truth, whom the world cannot receive, because it neither sees him nor knows him. You know him, for he dwells with you and will be in you" (John 14:15–17).

The Holy Bible

God had sixty-six books written, by men who devoted themselves to His will, and fourth-century believers compiled these books into one volume known as The Holy Bible.

Besides history and an array of true stories, the Bible explains God's will for us and answers many questions we may have concerning life and our role on Earth. It also paints a reasonable picture of His character and purposes. Referring to the Bible, Hank Hanegraaff wrote, "Without divine disclosure, we are but blind men grasping at the trunk of the proverbial elephant."[34]

The Bible condemns pride and often denounces viewpoints that folks like to support. Therefore, many people have rejected it or do not accept the Bible as the ultimate authority. To accomplish this, however, they must overlook the fact that the Bible is scientifically, archeologically, prophetically, and medically accurate—beyond reasonable doubt—even by honest, secular evaluations. It also includes many historical events that secular history sources have confirmed.

Over forty authors, from three continents, wrote the books of the Bible over a span of 1,500 years. Despite this diversity, these books complement each other remarkably well. Although skeptics have endeavored to destroy the Bible, it is still the most widely read book in the world.

In *Has God Spoken?*, Hank Hanegraaff refutes Bible critics and lays out facts illustrating the Bible's reliability. Dr. Don Bierle also records a thorough study of the Bible's integrity, which was instrumental in his conversion to Christianity, in the second chapter of

Surprised by Faith.

We have preserved many more ancient copies of the Bible that date much closer to the time of the recorded events than any other ancient text. This is especially true for the New Testament.

Scholar F. F. Bruce concluded, "The evidence for our New Testament writings is ever so much greater than the evidence for many writings of classical authors, the authenticity of which no one dreams of questioning. And if the New Testament were a collection of secular writings, their authenticity would generally be regarded as beyond all doubt."[35]

The "evidence" that the Bible is unreliable does not invalidate the Bible, but the critics' craving to invalidate the Bible produced the "evidence." Although the Bible frequently appears contradictory and is challenging to understand, a sincere and open-minded inspection can reveal an explanation to refute these discrepancies.

Let us examine two examples of apparent inconsistencies.

Abraham, whom the apostle James refers to as "the Friend of God," was married to his half-sister. Yet, the Bible clearly condemns sexual unions with close relatives (Deuteronomy 27:22 and Leviticus 18:6–9).

These scriptures seem to contradict each other, but let's investigate. Initially, there was no option but to marry a close relative. However, as time passed and human genes became more corrupted, it became necessary to establish laws against such unions. Abraham lived about five hundred years before God delivered the Law of Moses, recorded in Deuteronomy and Leviticus. In his era, it was yet acceptable to be married to his half-sister.

Another example concerns the father of Joseph, the husband of Jesus's mother. Matthew 1:16 states that Joseph's father is Jacob, but Luke 3:23 says he is the son of Heli.

Some study reveals that Matthew recorded Joseph's lineage, whereas Luke recorded Joseph's wife Mary's lineage.

Mary had no brothers. With no sons to preserve the family inheritance, the Jewish custom was for the oldest daughter's husband to become the son upon marriage to keep the family name. Thus, they could use Joseph's name in Mary's genealogy and refer to him as the son of Mary's father.

When reading God's Word with a receptive mind, we shall soon be convinced of its authority and the fact that it applies to us in the twenty-first century. The Bible itself proclaims in 1 Corinthians 2:14, "The natural person does not accept the things of the Spirit of God, for they are folly to him."

Although we can choose, we have a limited picture of what we are to accomplish in life. Therefore, it is God's plan for us to depend on Him and the Holy Bible for personal counsel and the instructions we need to accomplish His will.

God's People

Folks refer to those who devote their lives to God as Christians. Spectators in the first century gave them this name when they observed their unwavering devotion to Jesus Christ.

However, we use the term *Christian* much more casually today. In this twenty-first century, many Christians hold to the religion because it is what their parents believed, and deep inside, they may feel it is correct. But they resist the idea of God telling them how to live, and except for some Christian traditions and rituals, they mostly lead a secular life.

Over the centuries, Christianity has become increasingly corrupted. Many present-day Christians do not share the early church's zeal for Christ and the truth. Consequently, the modern Christian community has splintered into numerous groups that frequently contradict each other in their beliefs and interpretations of the Bible.

God never contradicts Himself. Undoubtedly, many Christians are, at least partially, incorrect concerning their idea of Christianity. This corruption of God's church is only possible because of our self-centeredness and low regard for God's principles. Due to satanic influence, many who think they are serving God are actually serving the devil.

As a result, many Christians and non-Christians alike have a warped concept of Christianity that leads millions to reject it. Friedrich Nietzsche said, "I will believe in the Redeemer when the Christian looks a little more redeemed."[36]

If accomplishing God's will is not our strongest desire, we are not what God considers a true Christian.

Note: Throughout this book, when I mention Christianity, I refer to authentic Christians who have not compromised Christ and the Bible.

Let us observe Ravi Zacharias's life.

Ravi's reputation as a renowned Christian minister and apologist was ruined when it was announced he had been involved in extensive immoral conduct for years. During his ministry, Ravi proclaimed the importance of truth and spoke against immorality.

So, what is the truth if a distinguished Christian and supporter of truth does not live in Christian truth?

Great question. The story about Ravi is sad. It shows that some Christians who are, by all appearances, on fire for the Lord may live hypocritical lives. Living a double life like this is a slap in God's face.

I mention this story to illustrate how easy it is for Christians to compromise on the truth if they do not wholly devote themselves to it. It takes considerable integrity to face the facts when we would rather ignore them, especially since ignoring the truth is so easy and popular these days.

Integrity is in short supply in this twenty-first century.

But here is a twist: I have experienced, through blogging with atheists, that skeptics are eager to discredit any who step on their toes. Any outspoken apologist will have enraged skeptics on their back who are desperate to discredit them. Considering the topics Ravi Zacharias was passionate about, I do not doubt the skeptics he angered would have paid dearly to set up a negative case about him.

In my research, I found the charges against Ravi quite biased. It appeared obvious that whoever was pushing these charges wanted to make him look as bad as possible. I also found that his wife and son are confident that he was innocent of these charges.

I acknowledge this negative story about Ravi Zacharias, in part or in whole, may be true. But it might not be.

Oh, the destruction and discomfort caused by the lies of folks who prefer any untruth that appears more convenient than its honest alternative. But have we not all played that game at some point or another?

* * * * *

Thankfully, not all Christianity is corrupted. Many sincere Christians across the globe enjoy the unspeakable security God has reserved for them. Folks who place every detail of their life in God's control have no reason to fear the unknown. Unger's Bible Dictionary defines Christian contentment as "That disposition of mind and restful quietness of the soul which, through Christ, is independent of outward circumstances."[37]

Can we expect any greater peace of mind than placing our lives in our Creator's hands? Frankly, multitudes spend a lifetime searching for the tranquility of spirit that sincere Christians possess.

Let me share a little about the Anabaptist environment I am in.

As conservative Anabaptists, we take much of the Bible's teachings literally. We will not serve in the military or participate in our country's politics. (Some of us vote in public elections, though many refuse to.) Our high moral standards do not tolerate divorce. Peace and friendship are common among us, although there certainly are exceptions. Anabaptists are also very hospitable. Many would give a bed and meal to almost anyone.

We do not tolerate TV, and the only movies many of us have watched were in museums, other than seeing glimpses here and there. This is not only because the church requests it, but it is what we prefer. We oppose the violence, immorality, and untruth that abounds on TV and in movies. Many Anabaptists also do not tolerate computer games and social media. We view interacting with family and friends—by conversing, playing games, and singing together—as a much better way to spend our free time.

Insurance is another thing for which Anabaptists see less need. With a caring community and a loving God by our side, we trust He will see that we have what it takes to endure the experience. When I was hospitalized in 2015, the deacon of my church told me, "Feel free to send me any bills you cannot cover." And that is what I did. When we have fire and storm losses, the community is quick to donate time and materials.

There are many large families among us. I would say our group averages about six or seven children per family. Some grandparents have around one hundred grandchildren. Yet many of these large family homes display a remarkable sense of serenity and love for each other.

But indeed, the me-infection is among us and is weakening our integrity, and church divisions frequently occur as issues arise and disagreements take their toll.

* * * * *

In *God in the Dark*, Os Guinness wrote:

> God is not only a person; He is the

supreme person on whom all personhood depends, not to speak of life itself and our entire existence. That is why to know Him is to trust Him, and to trust Him is to begin to know ourselves. That is why our chief end is to glorify God and enjoy Him forever. It is also why trusting God in the dark is so hard, and doubting God is so devastating. For when trust and dependence turn into doubt, it is as if the sun is eclipsed, the compass needle wavers without a north, and the very earth that was so solid moves as in an earthquake.[38]

Is all this turmoil and unrest in the world because we have lost our trust in God and begun doubting Him and His word? And could the reason we doubt Him be that we prefer not believing what He has to say due to the me-infection's influence?

Or maybe we are thinking, "A God who loves me is too good to be true."

At any rate, we will not experience God's love if we cannot step out and trust Him. It is living for God and His glory that will bring us the contentment we anticipate. As long as we keep God in our focus and give Him the reverence and respect He deserves, we will be satisfied.

> I sing the mighty power of God,
> That made the mountains rise;
> That spread the flowing seas abroad,
> And built the lofty skies.
> I sing the wisdom that ordained

The sun to rule the day;
The moon shines full at His command,
And all the stars obey.

I sing the goodness of the Lord,
That filled the earth with food;
He formed the creatures with His word,
And then pronounced them good.
"Lord, how Thy wonders are displayed,
Where-e'er I turn my eye:
If I survey the ground I tread,
Or gaze upon the sky!"

There's not a plant or flower below,
But makes His glories know;
And clouds arise, and tempests blow,
By order from Thy throne;
While all that borrows life from Thee
Is ever in Thy care,
And everywhere that man can be,
Thou, God, art present there.[39]

– Isaac Watts

4. Why Does God Allow Suffering?

> There are times when we see glimpses of God's ways,
> but not enough to allow us to make true conclusions
> about what He is doing and why. But we cannot resist
> jumping to conclusions anyway. Then, being insistent
> as well as inquisitive, we refuse to suspend judgment,
> and our wrong conclusions so misrepresent God that
> we end up doubting Him.[40] – Os Guinness

The amount of suffering in this world is unimaginable. If God is loving, why does He fill our lives with so much pain and heartache?

Keep in mind that much suffering is caused by people abusing their freedom of choice. Peter Kreeft points out,

After creation, He (God) declared that the world was "good." People were free to choose to love God or turn away from Him. However, such a world is necessarily a place where sin is freely possible—and, indeed, that potentiality for sin was actualized not by God, but by people. The blame, ultimately, lies with us. He did His part perfectly; we're the ones who messed up (Emphasis added).[41]

Many of our problems come from wanting our own way, and many more come from having it. God sees the complete picture of our lives and is far more capable of knowing what is best for us. His plan for us, in all aspects, is better than our plan for ourselves.

C. S. Lewis put it well when he wrote, "When we want to be something other than the thing God wants us to be, we must be wanting what, in fact, will not make us happy."[42]

We might ask God why He allows poverty, injustice, and all manner of suffering. But upon thinking it over, could God not even more justifiably ask us that question? A. W. Tozer wrote, "The cause of all our human miseries is a radical moral dislocation, an upset in our relation to God and to each other."[43]

God appointed that we must build a personal relationship with Him and rely on Him to help us make correct decisions. Only by God's help can we reach a condition of good. When we turn our backs on God's will, He uses suffering to draw us closer to Himself. Consequently, many of our problems result from humanity's poor decisions. Could we not replace these problems with desirable situations if we admitted our mistakes and took steps to correct them?

God deeply loves us, and it grieves Him to watch folks go through vast amounts of suffering that trace back to the poor choices they made because they insisted on their own way. These people are plodding through life without the unlimited benefits God freely offers all who heed His instructions.

Earth's climate was balmy and without extremes before the global flood (Genesis 6–7). This flood was likely the first natural disaster humanity had experienced. Because of mass corruption and indifference toward His will, God caused the flood to destroy the wicked people.

Earth now has a harsher environment, with more extreme weather, giving us more to think about so we spend less time getting into trouble. Have we not brought these severe conditions, including natural disasters, upon ourselves through our persistent stubbornness and disobedience? I do not mean disaster victims are worse than other people. I recognize humanity as a whole having "earned" these severe conditions; thus, humanity as a whole encounters them.

As for poverty and famine, are the wealthy not responsible for supporting the needy? If we all worked together and cared about others as much as we care about ourselves, we would provide for the less fortunate and educate them on supporting themselves. But is it not humanity's corruption and self-centeredness that hinder these processes?

Would poverty not dissolve if everyone loved others as much as they loved themselves? Let us each do what we can to make a difference.

Yes, not all suffering traces back to bad choices. Let us now examine six purposes that suffering fills:

#1. Suffering gets our attention.

Suppose you see your son walking the sidewalk beneath some construction workers high on a wall, and you see a hammer falling toward him from above. Would you not consider it wise to yank him to safety, even though you know such radical action would spark momentary anger?

Similarly, might God not use radical actions such as natural disasters, disease, and other adverse circumstances—out of profound affection—as a dramatic way of getting people's attention? I believe God sometimes uses suffering to alert us of our current dangerous position before worse things happen. If we do not alert to the danger the first time, will God not try getting our attention again, thus giving us still more pain and suffering?

My experience at my first job, as described in Chapter 2, is an example of God's corrective action. In Proverbs 3:11–12, Solomon states, "My son, do not despise the LORD's discipline or be weary of his reproof, for the LORD reproves him whom he loves, as a father the son in whom he delights."

If we had no pain, we would not see a need for God to lift our heavy burdens and prepare a heaven where we can eternally rest from evil. It is when God helps us through our problems that we can trust Him and feel certain of His existence. Patrick Morley stated, "Suffering compels us to seek the God that success makes us think we don't need."[44]

If early humanity had believed God's word and done what He told them, we would have far less pain now. But are we not just as stubborn as they were? God could hardly get us stiff-necked folks to associate with Him if He did not offer us relief from our problems.

God would gladly refine humanity to where it has fewer problems, but He only refines people who choose to be submissive to His correction. It is our choice to submit to God and enjoy the peace that comes with it, or insist on our own way and writhe in untold quantities of problems.

#2. Problems teach us lessons.

Suffering helps us become wise and can teach us critical lessons (Hebrews 12:5–11). It is our problems that are our teachers. Without problems, we would learn nothing; and the more problems we have, the more we can learn—that is, if we don't give up. Apostle Paul states in Romans 5:3-4, "We rejoice in our sufferings, knowing that suffering produces endurance, and endurance produces character, and character produces hope…"

As issues arise in my life, I try to consider what good might come from them. I do not remember having any problem for which I could not locate a worthy outcome. This practice of finding a purpose for my pain has helped me accept and even appreciate my problems.

Although we might have avoided some of our problems if we had behaved more wisely, many of these issues are unavoidable on our part. They are there mainly to fine-tune our character and teach us valuable lessons.

#3. Adversity can draw us closer to God.

Lee Rufener mentioned about tough times:

> There is no more effective avenue to teach us patience than the discipline of darkness, from which few saints are exempt.
>
> …There are times of persecution and

testing that are designed to bring saints unto the soul reckoning that only dark nights can minister unto.

...The dark night is the place where self-deception dies, and an intimate knowledge of God is birthed. It transitions us from loving God for the blessings He gives us to loving God for our relationship with Him and the communion that follows.[45]

In John 15, Jesus refers to himself as a vine, his followers as branches growing out of that vine, and his Father as the vinedresser. He mentions, "Every branch that does bear fruit he prunes, that it may bear more fruit" (John 15:2). Many problems we face are God's "pruning," which He is doing for our overall good that we might "bear more fruit."

Peter Kreeft says about Job's severe trials, "God didn't let Job suffer because he lacked love, but because he did love, in order to bring Job to the point of encountering God face to face, which is humanity's supreme happiness. Job's suffering hollowed out a big space in him so that God and joy could fill it."[46]

Think about it: Would there be Christians if there were no problems? Is it not our problems that show us our need for Christ and bring us to our knees?

#4. Disasters can bind us together.

Suffering can bring families and communities together if it is responded to correctly. Problems can pull relationships apart when we react in anger and blame others for our troubles. However, the same difficulties will draw us together when we respond with a caring attitude as we pray for each other and work together through challenging issues.

Many have witnessed how problems, ranging from community disasters to children's bumps and bruises, have strengthened relationships. No, we rarely conclude that we are glad the problem happened, but consider the benefits humanity has reaped from its troubles in this way over the ages.

#5. Pain can sometimes serve as a test.

Sometimes, problems may serve as tests to see how we react and reveal our maturity or education level.

If you suppose you have many more painful experiences than you deserve, I recommend reading the first and last chapters of Job. In a nutshell, Job was a godly man who endured severe suffering as a test of his faith. In the end, he passed the test and gained many benefits from the patience he demonstrated.

#6. Pain serves as a guardrail.

Pain's final significant role is to serve as a guardrail so we do not continually do destructive things. Imagine raising a child who could not feel pain. In *The Gift of Pain*, Dr. Paul Brand tells of an eleven-year-old girl he knew who lived a pathetic existence in an institution and had both legs amputated. Her only abnormality was that she felt no pain.

Imagine eating those delicious hamburgers until you

cannot swallow anymore because you do not feel pain. Does pain not also serve as a critical guide in many other aspects?

* * * * *

Everybody faces suffering as it fills these essential roles. But some problems, like rape and murder, have no merit. The people facing these problems are just victims of aggressive me-folk out to gratify their selfish desires. The lesson onlookers can learn from these problems is that living for one's own pleasure is devastating and horrible.

A skeptic once told me, "If God were all-powerful, he could work this system without suffering. The fact that we suffer proves that God is either not all-powerful or not all-loving."

Was that skeptic not merely trying to stuff God into his "basket"? Our empty "baskets" do not always prove anything. They might only illustrate our ignorance, or that we do not want to believe.

When we cannot see what good could come from our suffering, we do well to trust that God knows what is best for us. God operates on a vastly different level than we do, and we cannot expect to understand everything about how He functions. Isaiah 55:8–9 notes, "For my thoughts are not your thoughts, neither are your ways my ways, declares the LORD. For as the heavens are higher than the earth, so are my ways higher than your ways and my thoughts than your thoughts."

God desires that we allow our problems to fine-tune our character to what He wants of it and to steer us down the path He wants us to go. Apostle Paul mentions in Romans 5:3–4, "We rejoice in our sufferings, knowing that suffering produces endurance, and endurance produces character, and character produces hope."

Let me share some of my experiences as examples of how God sometimes guides us.

Oct. 1, 2024 – I was paying my toll-by-plate invoice from the PA Turnpike.

Upon thinking about it, I decided to get E-Z Pass to cut down on how much I have to pay. I filled out the online form, but when I clicked the final button to submit it, a note popped up about entering my credit card number again. My credit card number was wrong, so I fixed it and tried it again, and again, and again … but it refused to work.

I finally concluded, "Apparently, I am pursuing what God does not want me to do, and this is His roadblock to guide me to where He wants me to be."

I tried using different credit cards and account settings, and restarted my computer, but nothing worked. So, I eventually gave up on E-Z Pass and just paid the toll-by-plate bill, and it worked great—with the same credit card I had been trying earlier.

So, I conclude, "This is God's will for me at this time." I don't know why, but I don't need to know why.

Nov. 12, 2024 – Wesley, a blind friend

of mine, and I had a hard time getting his braille display connected to his laptop. We tried different chords and plugged it into my computer, but nothing. And yes, these devices had worked together flawlessly before.

Then I got an idea. I asked Wesley if the braille display is Bluetooth compatible, and he said, "Yes, but I do not use it because it does not work right."

I suggested, "Maybe this is God's way of telling you to use Bluetooth, and it will work now."

He said, "I can try." And it worked perfectly! He tried the thing that hadn't worked before, and it now works fine.

(Wesley later told me he is glad he had that connection problem because the Bluetooth connection works well, and he no longer has to deal with a cord.)

Nov. 30, 2024 – I brought my nail bag into the garage and piled its tools into my tool crate before cleaning the dirt out of it. I could not locate a sweeper or shop vac, so I shook the dirt out onto the concrete floor.

Then, when organizing my tools, I found that my screwdriver with interchangeable bits was missing the little bearing that holds the bit in place. I decided it would be worth looking through the dirt I had dumped out of the nail bag, which was still on the garage floor, and sure enough, I found the bearing!

It was not until I added this account to my diary that I thought of it: If I had found the sweeper and vacuumed out my nail bag, that bearing would have been lost forever.

Isn't it amazing how God guides those little details when we trust Him?

When we complain about our difficulties, we are underestimating God and His divine plan for us and only increasing our problems. We will feel much better about life's disappointments if we accept them as God-sent adjustments to our course. We can rise above our difficulties when we acknowledge God and allow Him to assist us. Should we not be thanking God for disciplining and refining us with suffering?

The saying goes, "What doesn't break you will strengthen you." In other words, the more we struggle, the more we will be worth once the struggle is over—if we live through it.

Friend, once you finally pull through the trial you are currently facing, you will be a gem, I'm sure, worth more than before you had those problems that made you feel like running out the door.

Also, God doesn't give us more than we can bear. He knows we can stand the trials He is putting us through. Let us trust that God knows what He is doing and has a worthy purpose for every tribulation He has in store for us. God intends to turn us into amazing aides for Him in His work.

It has also been said (I have paraphrased it a little.),

"If all the problems that you and your friends have were thrown on a pile for all to see, you would end up being glad you have the problems you have and do not need to deal with theirs." God has us tuned to bear the problems He has for us, and because we are not tuned to bear the trouble other people have, our issues are less of a problem for us than they would be for others.

I also want to point out that God's goal is for us to live above all pain and suffering in heaven. Suffering is temporary, with the critical God-ordained role of being an asset to us in this life. All pain has a purpose and lessons to be learned, although we might not put a finger on that purpose or lesson in this life.

Despite the heartaches they bring, pain and suffering are critical parts of our life. 2 Corinthians 4:17 promises, "For this light momentary affliction is preparing for us an eternal weight of glory beyond all comparison."

Another aspect I have considered is: As Christians, we rely on God to help us through our problems and comfort us in our distresses, just as a loving parent comforts their child. But skeptics have no such consolation. As a result, life's problems prove to be a much bigger issue to skeptics than they do to Christians. While Christians have a loving God to count on as they face life's challenges, skeptics must meet them on their own strength. I am sure I would also detest problems if that were the case for me, but with God by my side, I have nothing to fear.

Leon Horning suggests, "If truth, mercy, and knowledge of God are removed, there is nothing left to alleviate suffering. On the other hand, these three things are God's simple remedy for the ills of human-ity."[47]

In *How God Makes Men*, Patrick Morley shares, "Although you are not insulated from suffering, you are under God's protection while you suffer. God loves you very much, and you can lean on Him as you walk through it."[48]

I am confident you will receive consolation if you humbly and openly tell God how you feel about your problems. Not that God does not already know our situation, but we need to admit to Him how we feel and submit our will to His remedy. For myself, God does an incredible job of helping me cope with my problems when I request His help. I am confident He is anticipating doing the same for you.

Much human suffering is caused by man's poor choices; thus, a world without suffering would be without choice. Do you value personal choice? If you do, then you have better value suffering.

Wild pearls, which are highly valued and sought after, are produced by clams and oysters when sand gets under their shells. Instead of letting the grain of sand (their problem) bother them, they build a pearl around it and turn it into something precious. Should we not do the same with our problems?

All in all, problems are a privilege, and we really should thank God for them. If nothing else, we can at least trust that God knows what is best for all of us, and He knows our suffering will all be worth the pain in the end.

I am confident that in the end we will thank God for every trial He had us go through. So, let's start thanking Him for our problems, and we shall shortly feel better about the situation.

(To read more on this subject, check out Philip Yancy's book, *Where Is God When It Hurts?*.)

How firm a foundation, you saints of the lord!
Is laid for your faith in His excellent Word,
What more can He say than to you He has said,
Who unto the Savior for refuge have fled?

"Fear not, I am with Thee, O be not dismayed,
For I am thy God and will still give the aid;
I'll strengthen thee, help thee, and call thee to stand,
Upheld by my righteous, omnipotent hand.

"Went through the deep waters I call thee to go,
The rivers of sorrow shall not overflow:
For I will be with thee thy trouble to bless,
And sanctify to thee thy deepest distress.

"Went through fiery trials thy pathway shall lie,
My grace all-sufficient shall be thy supply;
The flames shall not hurt thee—I only design
Thy dross to consume and thy gold to refine.

"The soul that on Jesus hath leaned for repose,
I will not, I will not desert to his foes;
That's soul, though all hell shall endeavor to shake,
I'll never, no never, no never forsake."[49]

— Unknown

All things work for our good,
Though sometimes we can't see how they could.
Struggles that break our hearts in two
Sometimes blind us to the truth.
Our Father knows what's best for us;

His ways are not our own.
So, when your pathway grows dim,
And you just can't see him,
Remember, you're never alone!

He sees the master plan,
— He holds the future in His hands,
So don't live as those who have no hope.
All our hope is found in Him.
We see the present clearly,
He sees the first and last,
And like a tapestry,
He's weaving you and me,
To someday be just like Him.[50]
– Babbie Mason & Eddie Carswell

5. Satan, the Master of Deception

Give Satan an inch and he will
become a ruler.[51] – Unknown

Satan hates God and His creations. He broadcasts negative stories about God and His people to distract folks from seeing the blessings of being a Christian. He also actively tempts Christians to doubt God and His Word and pursue their personal desires over God's guidance. Regarding Satan, C. S. Lewis describes the earth as "enemy-occupied territory."

God created Satan, and because a creation cannot be as powerful as its creator, we know that Satan's authority is far inferior to God's. Although Satan is mighty, God is all-mighty and will always maintain control over him. As with Job, God has boundaries set that Satan cannot cross.

* * * * *

Following are some examples of the questions and lies Satan may place in the minds of Christians who struggle to let God control their lives. After each temptation, I have included the truth about that matter.

#1 "What would your friends think of you if you got caught up in only doing what God wants you to do?"

Committing ourselves to God's will shall significantly enhance our lives and is the most rewarding act a person can accomplish. When we encounter the contentment we have been seeking, we will consider it worth any negative thoughts our friends might have regarding our passion.

#2: "Real people are proud. This thing about humility is for cowards."

A large part of humility is about having enough backbone to stand against contrary pressures and face the facts, which is quite the opposite of a coward.

When we reach a state of humility, we will find it much more relaxing than the high maintenance of pride. Living a humble life is far more enjoyable. Proverbs 16:18 states, "Pride goes before destruction, and a haughty spirit before a fall."

We can also read in Proverbs 13:10, "Only by pride cometh contention: but with the well advised is wisdom." This verse affirms that there is no contention without pride. It also suggests that pride is contrary to wisdom.

Pride is the underlying cause of the me-infection and thus is responsible for most human suffering. C. S. Lewis pointed out, "It is pride which has been the chief cause of misery in every nation and every family since the world began."[52]

Satan wants people to be proud, for that is when he can control them. On top of that, he likes when folks are in misery.

#3: "You are eccentric, clumsy, and so full of errors. You're not popular, you're not good-looking, etc. It is unreasonable to think that God cares about you and how you live."

God had a purpose for every detail about us. He has a specific plan in mind for us and has equipped us with everything we need to accomplish what He wants us to do. A quote I saw the other week that put it well: "The world needs who you were made to be" – Joanna Gaines. [53]

Let's imagine, for a minute, that God was going to introduce the concept of a mammal to His helpers. First, He comes out with two eyeballs and a nose. Then He fetches baskets of bones and entrails, a box of teeth and toenails, jugs of blood, and bundles of skin and hair. His helpers might doubt whether this concoction would be worth anything, much less good to look at, until they see how all these strange parts fit together, each serving an essential role in a magnificent creature.

We might feel like our life looks just as confusing. But when we see the big picture, we will find ourselves thanking God for His patience and willingness to put up with our frustrations while He worked on this masterpiece that has our name attached.

#4: "You can't have any fun if you only do what God says. Such a lifestyle must be boring with all the restrictions that go with it."

God is a master of love and liberty. Surrendering to Him brings profound freedom, not bondage like Satan would have us believe. God is not a captor but a deliverer. He is not an oppressive tyrant but an affectionate friend. Truthfully, it is Satan who is a brutal suppressor of any who rejects God's offer of freedom.

God intends that we live righteously. Often, folks are discontent because they are not practicing right living. They are not living right because Satan is influencing their lives and doing all he can to deprive them of such a gratifying experience.

We will find life to be far more rewarding when we restrain ourselves from those self-indulgences that many people call fun. God makes sure His people are grateful for their effort in supporting Him by showering them with profound peace of mind.

As for restrictions, let us have a story:

Once, a toddler named Charlotte found a neatly decorated bar of soap that looked like a big piece of candy. It smelled delicious too. Charlotte decided she would like to eat it. Her mother saw what was happening and snatched the soap from her just in time.

Charlotte was upset, and she did not feel any better after her mother told her the soap would not taste as good as it looks. Charlotte thought, "I want to eat that big piece of candy. Mom just called it soap so I don't eat it." Thinking over it, she concluded, "I don't like being told what to do. I wanna do whatever I feel like."

The following week, Charlotte found the same bar of soap. Her mother was not around, so she took a big bite.

We must recognize that God has established restrictions for us out of love to protect us from destructive elements, as David G. Burkholder wrote, "Anything that God requires of us is for our benefit."[54]

Though we sometimes crave the prohibited, it does not pay to get arrogant, ignore the rules, and end up with a mouthful of soap. Satan will always be on our case, trying to entice us with the things we may not have. Had we not better surrender to God's boundaries, even when we do not understand their purposes?

Frankly, man shall never find sustained freedom in his impulsive pursuits. The more he feeds them, the hungrier they become, and they always lead toward a state of oppression. Satan likes to manipulate people's reasoning until they run headlong into captivity, looking for freedom.

Thankfully, the more we ignore these sensual desires, the more they lessen in appetite and fade to the corners of our minds. As our bond with God strengthens, His principles will influence our thinking patterns, and what Satan had us think was fun will gradually lose its appeal.

The thrill and adventure we crave is what we get after we surrender ourselves to God's will.

In my experience, I note that I would not have

had my three most fulfilling experiences of teaching
school, serving at Red Rock Refuge, and
administrating Windmill Workshop (each of which
contain its share of priceless adventure stories) if I
had been living for self and trying to get away with
as much as I could. At this point in my life, I can
testify that daily laying my life in God's hands, and
pursuing His will without exception, provide all the
thrill and adventure I could ever desire.

#5: "Do you really think you have time for all
that nonsense God is throwing at you?"

Naturally, we will find time for the things we
want to do. Dedicated Christians want to take time
for God and His work and find joy and contentment
in doing so. The more time we take for God, the
stronger our bond with Him gets, and the better we
understand His purposes.

* * * * *

Martin Wells Knapp wrote:

> As has been seen, Satan and his
> emissaries, disguised as "angels of
> light," by wrong impressions are ever
> seeking to ruin souls, and to divert
> God's children from their divinely
> appointed mission. He always shapes
> his methods to his victims, and whom
> he cannot openly allure he seeks to
> subtly deceive.
>
> He accomplishes his purpose with
> many impressions in a way something

like that by which we poison rats. We do not throw down a lot of strychnine and say, "Rats, eat it and die." We take just a little and mingle it with some meal so concealed that they will not suspect the poison, and then they eat the meal, and with it poison enough to cause their death. So Satan takes the meal of divine truth and mingles with it enough error to accomplish his purpose, and men eat and are betrayed.[55]

The Devil's Diary by Bobby Price, and *The Screwtape Letters* by C. S. Lewis, give detailed insight into how Satan may function. Of course, these books are just the authors' speculations, but they give the reader a lot to think about.

Some folks may find Satan's advertising too compelling and almost impossible to resist. Yes, Satan is an expert tempter, and he knows in what areas we are most likely to yield. Only by God's help can we defeat Satan.

The Bible promises, "No temptation has overtaken you that is not common to man. God is faithful, and he will not let you be tempted beyond your ability, but with the temptation he will also provide the way of escape, that you may be able to endure it" (1 Corinthians 10:13).

Do temptations not serve as powerful educators, as they fine-tune our character and teach us invaluable lessons in patience and the importance of relying on God?

God can destroy all His enemies and will do that in the end. Here is a potential reason God has let His adversaries tempt us humans for now:

I believe God uses this vast array of evils to tune and test us humans, picking out folks who are dedicated to truth and then educating and fine-tuning them to fill the role He has chosen for them. God may also use these trials to test us to see how we respond to tribulations and hold up under adverse pressures.

Nothing beats the gratification and security of experiencing God's smile of approval. Indeed, my friend, we will never regret standing up against Satan and obeying God.

> Break the cord of sin that binds;
> Flee from Satan's slavery.
> From the Lord gain aid divine,
> And sufficient bravery.
> Fight all wrong with zeal and find
> Freedom from oppression.
> Sweet reward and peace of mind
> Will be your expression.
> – M. Z. Hurst

6. Our Spiritual Allegiance

Choose this day whom you will serve. … But as for me and my house, we will serve the LORD. – Joshua 24:15

We were born with a self-centered (carnal) nature, which is the spirit of Satan, that inclines us to think and desire wrong things and leads us to greed, rebellion, and dishonesty.

As we mature, God's spirit of love and integrity starts calling for our attention. The spirit of God (the Holy Spirit), of which our conscience is a part, places thoughts and convictions in the heart of everyone mature enough to make their own decisions. If we accept this spirit's guidance, It will make Itself at home in our lives.

Let us look at what David G. Burkholder says about the Holy Spirit in *The Heart of God*:

> If we are children of God, the Holy Spirit is our Comforter, our Guide, our Companion. He is our God within! His gentleness creates the possibility for a close relationship. His presence is God's claim on our lives… When He is

allowed to be the full representation of God within, He will cause our spirit to grow and blossom as He did for the psalmist (referring to King David) (Emphasis added).[56]

God wants us to choose to follow Him over living the way of our original inclinations, which will help us be more committed to Him in the end. If we were born with God's spirit dominating our lives, and would not have suffered the discontentment one has without It, would we not then find it easier to neglect devotion to It?

God and Satan place thoughts and feelings into our minds, similar to ads we might see in magazines or on billboards. Sometimes, their messages are relentless and urgent, like a flashing sign. These subtle messages are frequently not thought of as coming from a spiritual source.

Perhaps you remember a thought, quite removed from what you had been thinking, bursting into your head so sudden and bold-like that you wondered, "Why did I think that?" Or maybe a notion insisted you think about it, even though you continually brushed it aside. Such instances are the workings of these spiritual powers.

You probably remember that acute dread and resistance you felt when you first heard that you should surrender your life to God. That emotion is from Satan as he desperately tries to draw you away from the only Source of true peace and fulfillment. And you are acquainted with guilt, which generally comes from God.

These authorities also give us messages through the material we read and the speech of people around us.

Martin Wells Knapp thoroughly explains this subject in his book *Impressions*.

We have the ability and authority to accept or reject any thought presented to us by God or Satan.

So, here we are, influenced by Satan's spirit and attracted by the Spirit of God, both of which tirelessly pursue us. Ultimately, we have a few routes before us from which to choose.

#1. We can reject the evil force and ask the Holy Spirit to rule our lives. God shall grant us our request, and we can arise renewed and ready for what He has in store for us.

Satan will continue to entice us to serve our selfish nature instead, but if we have committed ourselves to God, He will help us. As our bond with God grows, Satan will slink farther away; however, he will never give up, and we shall fight this enemy until our death. Nonetheless, God will have His hand on our shoulder, so to speak, and we can forever rejoice in our decision to follow Him.

#2. We might choose not to decide or to wait a while before surrendering to God. In this case, Satan will do his best to ensure we find no convenient time to change our allegiance. Also, God does not promise us another day of opportunity. Nevertheless, if we push off this decision, the Holy Spirit will keep pursuing us as long as we live until we surrender to Its control.

#3. If we are tired of God bothering us and want to serve ourselves without Him reminding us of another way, we might—perhaps only subconsciously—desire God's spirit to go away and leave us alone. God's spirit will then retreat, and Satan shall wrap his fingers around us and drag us deeper into his dark kingdom.

If we have seen the Holy Spirit at work in folks around us, we will be much more likely to answer Its calling and devote our lives to It ourselves. On the other hand, if we have never seen God's spirit function in the lives of our associates, we are much less likely to commit ourselves to It. After all, is it not easier to buy something if we see it demonstrated?

Romans 1 describes the situation Satan has gotten many people into:

> Therefore God gave them up in the lusts of their hearts to impurity, to the dishonoring of their bodies among themselves, because they exchanged the truth about God for a lie and worshiped and served the creature rather than the Creator, who is blessed forever! Amen ...
>
> And since they did not see fit to acknowledge God, God gave them up to a debased mind to do what ought not to be done. – Romans 1: 24–25, 28

Although the most attractive path leads to fear and hopelessness, God's way leads to a satisfied mind and substantial peace and joy.

You can choose to give your service
To the One who paid the price,
Or the one who wants your service
To do wrong and keep you tied.

You must know whom you are serving,
When you hide yourself from right;
There's a record kept in heaven,
Hidden things are brought to light.

Count the cost with Christ the Savior,
Count the cost of wasted life;
If you choose to Lord your Maker,
You will say 'twas worth the price.[57]
– John Esh

The Contentment Dilemma

7. Humanity's Fall and Liberation

The restless sensation so widespread today is the
subconscious awareness that we have transgressed a
divine law and stand guilty before a God of
uncompromised justice. – M. Z. Hurst

The Fall of Man

Initially, there was nothing imperfect or negative
on Earth besides the devil. However, Genesis 2 and
3 record how the first human couple took their lives
into their own hands and made the first tracks down
this corrupted road we walk on today.

The moment Adam and Eve disobeyed God's
command and ate the forbidden fruit, their eyes
were opened and their innocence vanished as they
took on the knowledge of evil. It appears to me that
we also are innocent before receiving the knowledge
of evil when we make our first conscious choice to
do wrong, though I could be wrong about that.

God allows us to know which things are evil and
which are good. However, if continually ignored,
this instinctive moral code can diminish and
eventually expire.

You may think, "But I am a good person."

You may be good compared to some folks. Nonetheless, since humanity has an inborn nature of curiosity and impulsiveness, and a tendency to make decisions without seeking God's counsel, there is no room for continual perfection from birth. "For all have sinned, and come short of the glory of God" (Romans 3:23).

Question 7: Why did God make it so hard for us that no human can live an entirely sin-free life?

A Few Facts About Sin

Satan wants us to think some sins are not as bad as others, but we do well to acknowledge that all sin is equally wrong and will make us children of hell. Some wrongs are not as obvious and have less negative impact than others, but they do not make a person any less of a sinner in God's eyes.

Anything more important to us than our connection with God is an idol. Thus, deliberately transgressing God's will renders us idolaters, on the same level of wrongness and damnation as the Israelites who openly worshipped Baal.

Satan will not let you acknowledge this truth if he can help it, for deception is a significant handle of his. He is quite successful in getting folks to do "little" wrongs with the excuse that "At least it is not as bad as what some people are doing." But that "little" sin gets folks in Satan's grip just the same.

As long as we pursue things God disapproves of, we shall lead a restless and miserable life.

Is God not deeply hurt when we willfully sin or know we have done wrong but choose to cover it up instead of admitting it and apologizing? And what about doing questionable things with the mindset of, "It might not be sin, and I would hate to refrain from it only to find out later that it would have been alright after all."?

These actions and attitudes are like slapping God in the face and stating, "I don't care about what you think!". How He longs to gather these individuals as a hen gathers her chicks under her wings, but they would not.

Thankfully, God is willing to forgive us for slapping Him in the face and is eager to show us a better way.

Some folks may view God's guidelines for living as heartless persecution, but in reality, these guidelines better compare to guardrails on the road to peace and happiness. It is out of His deep love for us that God offers these guides. He knows that staying on that road is the only way to reach the serenity and contentment we desire.

I also want to share a point that Ravi Zacharias brings out concerning the effect of sin:

> Someone has rightly said that the worst effect of sin is shown, not in suffering or in bodily defacement, but rather in "the dis-crowned faculties, the unworthy loves, the low ideals, the

brutalized and the enslaved spirit."

Think of that, phrase by phrase:

Dis-crowned faculties: all the brilliance and creative genius we have within humanity, and yet we stoop to such base pursuits.

Unworthy loves: practices we ought to despise, yet we stoop to such depraved pursuits (pornography, violence, hate, profanity).

Low ideals: we ought to set our vision for things that are noble, yet we spend time and effort on the ignoble.

The brutalized and enslaved spirit: We sink deeper and deeper into bad habits till we enslave ourselves. This is the worst form of slavery of which we so seldom speak.[58]

God's Plan for Our Liberation

After Adam and Eve sinned, God promptly started on a deliverance plan so we could obtain complete forgiveness for our offenses. Thanks to His mercy, God planned that His own Son—the only person to live a perfect life—would die to take the blame for the sins of humanity.

Jesus, our long-anticipated Savior, faced all the problems and temptations man faces, but he never sinned. C. S. Lewis describes him as "...one man that really was what all men were intended to be."[59]

Despite his blamelessness, Jesus' own people rejected and crucified him out of envy for his power and fame. But Jesus arose from the dead three days after his crucifixion, thus proving his ability to dismiss our penalty of damnation. (Accounts of this story are recorded in Matthew 27 & 28 and Luke 22–24.)

Peter Kreeft said about Jesus:

> Jesus is there, sitting beside us in the lowest places of our lives, … Are we broken? He was broken, like bread, for us. Are we despised? He was despised and rejected of men. Do we cry out that we can't take any more? He was a man of sorrows and acquainted with grief. Do people betray us? He was sold out himself. Are our tenderest relationships broken? He too loved and was rejected. Do people turn from us? They hid their faces from him as from a leper.
>
> Does he descend into all of our hells? Yes, he does. From the depths of a Nazi death camp, Corrie Ten Boom wrote, "No matter how deep our darkness, he is deeper still." He not only rose from the dead, he changed the meaning of death and therefore of all the little deaths—the sufferings that anticipate death and make up parts of it.[60]

Norman Troyer shared, about Jesus' crucifixion, "To this day, a degree of mystery lies behind this life-for-death transaction. We do not believe (as many do) that Jesus was punished for our sins. Instead, 'Jesus paid it all.' He did not pay a penalty for us; rather, He purchased our redemption. Praise His name! Yes, Jesus purchased our redemption; but that will not benefit us until we believe it and pursue God's will in true repentance of our sins."[61]

Many have found it in their best interest to write off Jesus' death and resurrection as a myth. You'll find ample evidence, however, that this story was widely circulated only a few years after it was said to happen, while many eyewitnesses were still living. Abdu Murray wrote, "We may prefer a particular view about Jesus because it provides us with comfort, but what we need is the truth."[62]

The temple curtain, which tore in two pieces when Jesus died, had separated the people from God's presence in The Most Holy Place of the temple. In that era, the common people were considered unworthy of being in God's presence. The tearing of that curtain signifies that God now invites all people to freely experience His presence.

Thanks to His unconditional love for humanity, God refuses to give up on us. Part of His redemption plan is to make us feel incomplete when we neglect our relationship with Him. God places the craving for something more in our hearts when we fail to observe His will and credit Him His due position to awaken us to our error and the malfunction in our lives. This longing also helps attract us to the lives of those we can see live more peacefully, making it possible for others to draw us closer to God.

Long ago, at a place called Mount Calvary,
Died a man who now means so much to me.
Though I've never been there,
Still the shame I must share;
For it all came by fault of sinful man.

Guilty, I stand before Him guilty,
And I have no defense to stand by me.
Guilty, I stand before Him guilty,
But God's love and compassion set me free.[63]
— Clarence E. Jones

The Contentment Dilemma

8. The Eternal Effects of Our Choices

And, behold, I come quickly; and my reward
is with me, to give every man according as
his work shall be. – Revelations 22:12 (KJV)

God shall judge each of us according to our deeds: "God's righteous judgment will be revealed. He will render to each one according to his works: to those who by patience in well-doing seek for glory and honor and immortality, he will give eternal life; but for those who are self-seeking and do not obey the truth, but obey unrighteousness, there will be wrath and fury" (Romans 2:5–8).

God shall reveal and proclaim every truth about us: "Nothing is covered up that will not be revealed, or hidden that will not be known" – Luke 12:2.

God will welcome the righteous, who sought His forgiveness and endeavored to live by His standards, to live in His presence, forever perfectly content (Isaiah 64:4). And because He is good, God will demand justice for any who do not repent of their transgressions. He will sentence folks who disregard

Question 8: According to Genesis, when God created everything, he declared it was 'good.' Obviously, God created hell. But how could he possibly think that hell is good?

His doctrine to a pit of unspeakable misery (Psalms 9:17, Revelations 20:10).

God is all-knowing and will not sentence any innocent people to hell. He is also thorough in revealing Himself to the open mind. Romans 1:20 suggests the souls God condemns to hell will, by that time, know they deserve every bit of the pain they feel.

In *The Great Divorce,* C. S. Lewis points out, "All that are in Hell, choose it. Without that self-choice, there could be no Hell."[64]

We may wonder why God does not just save everybody, but remember, we are not robots. We must choose for ourselves whether we will submit to God's will.

Question 9: What about the people who live a virtuous life but do not identify with Christianity? Will they go to hell just because they were not a Christian?

Skeptics might reason that hell is cruel. If killing or tormenting others is morally wrong, how can God justify sentencing people to Hell? And why would a loving God torture his enemies?

God is not under the moral law, and He will deal out justice.

Let us look at how J. P. Moreland describes hell:

Make no mistake: hell is punishment—but it's not a punishing. It's not torture. The punishment of hell is separation from God, bringing shame, anguish, and regret. And because we will have both body and soul in the resurrected state, the misery experienced can be both mental and physical. But the pain that's suffered will be due to the sorrow from the final, ultimate, unending banishment from God, his kingdom, and the good life for which we were created in the first place. People in hell will deeply grieve all they've lost.

Hell is the final sentence that says you refused regularly to live for the purpose for which you were made, and the only alternative is to sentence you away for all eternity. So it is punishment. But it's also the natural consequence of a life that has been lived in a certain direction.[65]

There will be no alternative to these two final destinations, nor will there be partiality (1 Peter 1:17). As ignorance of the law is no excuse in court, it is also reasonable to believe God will hold us responsible for discovering His will for us.

C. S. Lewis again pointed out, "There are only two kinds of people in the end: those who say to God, 'Thy will be done,' and those to whom God says, in the end, 'Thy will be done.'"[66]

Please keep in mind that the time will come when we all face reality. I hope when that time comes, you will not have a part with those who will cry bitter tears.

Thanks to Christ, our lives can have meaning. None of us need to experience hell if we accept God's offer of forgiveness and commit ourselves to His will.

In the day of all days,
When the world shall be judged,
And the chaff from the wheat
Shall be thoroughly fanned,
Then the righteous shall shine
As the stars in the sky,
And their places shall be
At the Savior's right hand.

But the wicked who will
Not repent and believe,
And will never live up
To the Master's command,
Shall be placed on the left,
As unworthy to be
With the children of God
At the Savior's right hand.

We are journeying on
To eternity now,
On the bank of death's Jordan,

We sometime shall stand!
Shall we fear to pass over
The dark rolling flood,
Lest our portion be not
At the Savior's right hand?

If our Shepherd He is,
And we follow His call,
He will lead us safe home
To that beautiful land:
And with crowns on our brows
And with branches of palm,
We shall ever abide
At the Savior's right hand.[67]
– Eden R. Latta

The Contentment Dilemma

9. Analyzing the Facts

Much of our difficulty as seeking Christians stems
from our unwillingness to take God as He is and
adjust our lives accordingly.[68] – A. W. Tozer

When your will is enslaved to anything, the first step to
free will is freely admitting your bondage. ... To win back
our free will, we must begin with humble honesty and by
realigning any deception in us with truth.[69] – Steve Simms

How can we expect God to place His wealth in our
hands if we are still clutching self-esteem? – M. Z. Hurst

Don't we all desire to lead a satisfying life in
which we secure the long-term contentment we have
always wanted?

As previously mentioned, a solution exists for
each desire we might have. When we are hungry, we
can eat food. The solution to thirst is drinking water,
and companionship solves loneliness.

We are familiar with guilt, for which the solution
is sincere repentance. And as for that persistent
apprehension in our lives, the solution is absolute
surrender to God, which leads to untold peace and
tranquility. The only escape from the confusion and
turmoil that saturates the world is to lay down our

self-will in complete humility and submission to the One who created us.

In the last chapter of Ecclesiastes, Solomon shares his conclusion of what we should do in this life: "Fear God and keep his commandments, for this is the whole duty of man. For God will bring every deed into judgment, with every secret thing, whether good or evil" (Ecclesiastes 12:13–14).

When we unconditionally surrender ourselves and commit the rest of our life to God's will, the benefits we reap shall exceed our greatest hopes. On the other hand, if we do not surrender our will, it shall eventually destroy us.

Our life compares to a vast maze with many appealing passages and much controversy over which way is best. Our view is dangerously limited, and of ourselves, we will lose our way. Only with God's help will we reach the desired location, for only He sees the big picture and knows where each passage leads.

Yes, unconditional surrender is indeed a frightening thought. One day, when U-Haul's area field manager came into the bike shop and U-Haul dealership where I worked, he said, "Hello Marcus, I have something for your next book." As I pulled out my notebook, he continued, "Your most gratifying rewards are hiding behind your maximum fears."

He told me, "A friend of mine told me that one. He liked to illustrate how first-time skydivers often fight a lot of fear before their first jump. But the experience is so gratifying that afterward they wonder why they ever feared it."

You know, friend, that describes committing one's life to God's will. Dr. Dennis Swanberg wrote, "Everybody resists God at one time or another, and so will you. But as you mature, you should realize that when it comes to God's instructions, it's better to be teachable than headstrong."[70]

Satan will do everything he can to keep us from surrendering. One of his methods is to convince folks that God does not care about them. The Bible plainly states that God loves us, so if we think God does not love us, we do not believe God and the Bible. We will not submit to a God we do not trust. Fear keeps us from trusting and surrendering, but "perfect love casts out fear" (1 John 4:18). The more we understand God's love for us, the easier it will be to yield to Him.

Upon thinking about it, one will find nothing to be gained by not surrendering their life to God's will.

Since my unconditional surrender, I have noted that pursuits such as pride, immorality, the craving for money, and the desire for that trophy buck, etc, are indeed very foolish. It is through Satan's blinding that humanity can lower itself to such base pursuits. Scripture acknowledges, "He (Satan) has blinded their eyes and hardened their heart, lest they see with their eyes, and understand with their heart, and turn, and I would heal them" (John 12:40, Emphasis added).

If people caught up in these sensual activities

could only see the foolishness and ignorance of these pursuits. Wealth and living for oneself do not bring people peace. In fact, these have been the principal players behind most strife and severed relationships. Ultimately, pursuing the truth will be our most gratifying line of action. Only God's smile on our lives can grant us that inner fulfillment we crave. With God's approval, the poorest individual can be content; without it, even the famed celebrity must be (at least inwardly) restless and apprehensive.

In *The Pursuit of God*, A. W. Tozer wrote, "The sinner prides himself on his independence, completely overlooking the fact that he is the weak slave of the sins that rule his member. The man who surrenders to Christ exchanges a cruel slave driver for a kind and gentle Master whose yoke is easy and whose burden is light."[71]

Ravi Zacharias wrote, "Dear friend, may you know today that the freedom to have peace without begins with the freedom from evil within."[72]

When we surrender to God, acquire His forgiveness, and pursue what He asks of us, we will feel like we are on a team with Him. The supreme sense of security we shall enjoy when we submit ourselves to God's principles will surpass all our expectations.

Being a Christian includes functioning as God's personal associate and representative on Earth. What a privilege! How exciting to be communicating with the creator of the universe and working under His supervision!

Masses are fleeing from the very Source of inner security and peace of mind they desire. These people are ramming themselves into cactus after cactus, so to speak, with their self-centered living, and many are taking drugs, in some form or other, to dull the pain they feel. All the while, they wonder why they aren't happier since they are freely doing what they want.

We do best to accept responsibility for our problems and realize that our pride and self-will are our worst enemies.

When we discover we are going in the wrong direction, turning around is the smartest way to our destination. C. S. Lewis wrote, "There is nothing progressive about being pig-headed and refusing to admit a mistake. And I think if you look at the present state of the world, it is pretty plain that humanity has been making some big mistakes. We are on the wrong road. And if that is so, we must go back. Going back is the quickest way on."[73]

I well remember when I initially took this step, my ego dreaded being humiliated, and Satan reminded me that he thought it was a cowardly thing to do. It was difficult to swallow my pride and ignore Satan's opinion, but the resulting unspeakable joy was certainly worth the effort. "For He (God) satisfies the longing soul, and the hungry soul He fills with good things" (Psalms 107:9).

Calvin Horst described the situation well when he noted, "How many of us want to make life and eternity miserable for ourselves? What about for

God and others? If not, are we willing to accept the road that leads to a happy win-win for everyone?"[74]

* * * * *

Surrendering to God is not something to merely test. It is a life commitment. If we attempt to be in God's will only temporarily to see if we like it, our commitment is not unconditional; thus, it will not yield the desired results.

I also want to clarify that total submission will not immediately solve all our problems. It will be a process that will likely take years to complete, but humility and surrender to God's will are the keys to starting that process.

We will need to surrender to God over and over. Heaven is not something we can easily achieve; it will be a lifelong battle that will produce many scars. The devil will continue tempting us, the struggle for truth and right will be fierce, and the Bible warrants that all Christians shall face some form of persecution (2 Timothy 3:12).

Sometimes these trials will lure our eyes off God and what He has done for us, and we may question if our commitment to Him is truly worth the effort. When this happens, getting our focus back on our Lord will always be the solution.

All in all, submitting to God will bring us the highest level of fulfillment we shall ever encounter. Mark Hatfield testified, "Following Jesus Christ has been an experience of increasing challenge, adventure, and happiness. He is totally worthwhile.

How true are His words: 'I am come that they might have life, and that they might have it more abundantly.' (John 10:10)"[75]

A Christian's relationship with God compares to a small boy and his dad who need to climb a steep mountain. The boy finds it much easier when his dad is with him to hold his hand, pull him over the steep spots, and carry him when the trail is rough. And so it is with our heavenly Father. In fact, without His help we will not reach our desired destination. It may also be worth noting that the more we surrender ourselves to God's aid, the more He can help us.

It is not worth the thrill
To step out of God's will;
Despite all the glitter
It will not fulfill.
Your emotions will grill,
While your spine has a chill.
It will constantly feel
Like you're going uphill.

When you walk in God's ways
You'll step out of the haze,
And with confident strides
You'll abandon the maze.
Your fear will be razed,
And your eyes, they will blaze
With notable gladness,
And passionate praise.
                    – M. Z. Hurst

10. The Initial Step of Surrender

Unless our relationship with God is right, no
amount of peace is possible. – John M. Drescher

As I live, declares the Lord GOD, I have no pleasure
in the death of the wicked; but that the wicked turn
from his way and live: turn ye, turn ye from your evil
ways; for why will ye die? – Ezekiel 33:11 KJV

The most crucial step toward a working relationship with God is commonly known as the new birth
experience. Let us examine five conditions we must
meet to encounter the new birth and the peace of
mind that accompanies it.

#1. We must believe in God. Below is what we
need to believe about God:

(a) God loves us unconditionally and truly
believes in us.

(b) Jesus Christ was the only human who never
sinned, and he allowed himself to be cruelly
murdered to take the place of the punishment we
deserve, and then he arose from the dead.

(c) God will forgive and forget all our regretted
offenses upon our sincere request.

#2. We must recognize that we have wronged

God.

#3. We must genuinely regret all our sins and desire to be free from them.

Repenting of our sins does us no good if we are not willing to repent of all of them. This is not about regretting our sins merely because we got tired of them, but because they transgress God's divine will. We shall not receive His forgiveness if we are unwilling to sincerely seek God's help to avoid sin.

#4. We must surrender ourselves to God. Unless we have an attitude of total submission, God will not forgive our sins. Jesus says, "So therefore, any one of you who does not renounce all that he has cannot be my disciple" (Luke 14:33).

Our money, family, and everything we own, including ourselves and our talents, never were ours—they are God's. God possesses the entire universe. (Psalms 24:1–2.) In all truth, we have nothing to offer God besides the complete resignation of our will, and that is all God requires. With our continued surrender, God can carve out a saint of spectacular majesty.

But do we not tend to claim sole ownership of things we think are within our control? The sooner we give everything back to God that is His the better off we will be.

#5. We must forgive those who wronged us. Matthew 6:15 points out, "If you do not forgive others their trespasses, neither will your Father forgive your trespasses." I heard it said already that holding a grudge is like picking up a hot coal to throw at someone—you are the one who gets hurt. Unforgiveness never does anyone good; it only destroys. It is just another one of Satan's foolish ideas with which he tempts humanity.

#6. We must ask God to forgive and forget our sins. God will not pardon an offense we do not regret. But if we have forgiven all who have offended us and request forgiveness in genuine faith, humility, and remorse, God will grant it to us.

To pray, it is helpful to find a quiet place that provides minimal distractions. I find that trying to communicate with God is ineffective if my mind is wandering around and not focused on my conversation with Him. Is it not a challenge to converse with someone who is not paying attention?

Heartfelt prayer is comparable to having a one-on-one conversation with God. It is not just a letter thrown on God's desk with a million others in hopes that ours is one of the small percentage He opens. God hears our prayers as though we were standing before Him and had His full attention. Our prayers, humility, and surrendered will are indeed precious to God. Of a certainty, the well-being of humanity is His highest priority.

God knows our thoughts, so when we think what is on our hearts, He understands. The words we process for God to hear need to be an accurate interpretation of our inner desires. It will not help to mechanically run words past God as though they were a magic formula without feeling that way in our hearts.

Steve Simms has some words of wisdom concerning the Christian conversion:

> The worst condition a person can be in is to think they are saved when they are not. (See Revelations 3:15–19.) Christianity is not just knowing about God but actually personally knowing Him. If I think I am saved when I am not, will I not settle into a false sense of religious security based on my knowledge of Jesus? Might I not subconsciously let that knowledge take the place of a humble and growing relationship with him?

Here is Simms' testimony, which also describes my experience:

> The more acquainted I am with the living Jesus, the more I realize that my knowledge about him is rather sketchy. The more I love him and surrender to his will, the less need I feel to try to figure out all the theological details about him. Instead, I prefer to bask in his presence and get lost in his splendor and wonder.
>
> I continually invite the Holy Spirit to lead me so I can know, experience, surrender to, and obey the risen Jesus better. I regularly experience the beatitude: "Blessed are those who

hunger and thirst for righteousness, for they shall be satisfied" (Matthew 5:6).

Many times, when I decide to get everything clear between God and me, I start by praying, "Search me, oh God, and know my heart: try me and know my thoughts: And see if there be any wicked way in me, and lead me in the way everlasting." (Psalms 139:23-24 KJV). A high level of divine serenity envelopes me, and I soon find myself entirely satisfied.

In the past few years, I have often experienced God's presence and assurance that I am right where He wants me to be, which is clearly worth the effort it takes to surrender to Him. If connecting with God brings such contentment to my life, I do not doubt it will prove equally worthwhile to you.

* * * * *

If you have sincerely, and in complete surrender, asked God to forgive you, then He has forgiven you. Thank Him for it. Like us, God enjoys being praised and respected. In fact, because He longs to associate with us, God built a desire to worship into our intellect. If we fail to reverence God, will we not find a substitute?

Worshipping God is essential for all Christians and can be done through prayer, singing, and attending worship services. These actions, however, mean nothing to God when our worship does not include dedicating our lives to His principles.

In the Bible, God often refers to Christians as His children. We ought to think of ourselves as small children in God's family and to think of God as our father. As Christians, we are members of God's family; we are His private aides and must devote ourselves to performing His will.

As Christians, we will discover that we no longer feel comfortable with the ways of common society. We will feel much more secure in a sound Christian environment. Christians function best in a group where they can provide vital support for each other. I highly recommend locating a sincere group of Christians with whom to associate. Joining a sincere Christian church will include water baptism as a symbol of our commitment to God and His will.

When we ask God to help us become better individuals, we might be satisfied after a few improvements, but God intends to make us into something we had never imagined. We might be content just to be decent people, but God wants to make us first-rate saints.

Friend, never again believe Satan when he tries to tell you that surrendering to God brings oppression. Indeed, Apostle Paul was not exaggerating in Philippians 4:7 when he described the peace of God as "passing all understanding".

Oh, the shackles of sin,
How they weighed me down.
Death laughed in my face,
Said I was gonna drown.
But God's mercy and grace
Were right there for me.

And Jesus' saving blood
Paid the price for me!

Now I have a new hope,
And no longer am bound
By the chain of defeat
That was dragging me down!
God said, "Take My hand,
I will see you through.
My love will never fail,
I'll be here for you."
– Unknown Author

The Contentment Dilemma

11. Overcoming Iniquity's Bondage

The only way to overcome a passion for
sin is with an overwhelming passion for
righteousness.[76] – David W. Hegg

As Christians, should we not be passionate about rising above sin and doing only what God wants? And let us remember that we are not resisting sin merely for our own sake and reputation, but for God's sake, that His name and reputation be preserved and exalted.

I think of sin's bondage as an addiction, for we know it is wrong and want to stop, but continue sinning as though we cannot help it. People who rise above sin will no longer consciously do wrong, and when they catch themselves doing or thinking wrong, they will promptly stop, repent, and make restitution instead of trying to hide the act. Thus, they are in control of their life instead of sin controlling them.

Let us analyze eight actions that will help us overcome iniquity's grip on our lives:

#1. First, we must admit that we have sinned, as 1 John 1:9-10 points out: "If we confess our sins, he is faithful and just to forgive us our sins and to cleanse us from all unrighteousness. If we say we have not sinned, we make him a liar, and his word is not in us."

#2. We must believe that God is eager to help us rise above our failures and live by His standards.

#3. We must surrender to God unconditionally, to where we will do whatever He asks. Is God's will a top priority in your life? Let me assure you, you will not rise above sin any other way. Sin happens when we choose to ignore God's will.

#4. As Christians, we need to hate sin and treat it as entirely off-limits. Why do prisoners obey when they do not want to and do not climb over the prison fence? It is because painful consequences are sure, and such actions only hinder in obtaining freedom.

When we view sin as off-limits and as regretful as climbing over an electric prison fence our temptations will dramatically lessen. It helps to see evil as God sees it—as utter foolishness and ignorance.

We must build an enthusiastic hatred for wrong actions and attitudes and train ourselves to not even consider doing it. We need to remember that there is no sin we would not eventually regret.

What if something is not a sin? Does that mean we may do it if we want?

We can agree that it would not be a sin to spit on the kitchen floor and then clean it up. But should we freely spit on floors because it is not a sin? We do well to keep in mind: If we would be ashamed to discuss with God an action we did or a thought we entertained, then we should avoid doing it, whether or not it is a sin.

#5. We must ask God to help us overcome temptation. Dr. Reuben A. Torrey states, "The reason why many fail in the battle is because they wait until the hour of battle. The reason why others succeed is because they have gained their victory on their knees long before the battle came. ... Anticipate your battles, fight them on your knees before temptation comes, and you will always have victory."[77]

Dr. Torrey worded that stronger than I would have, but I think he has a point. We do well to take every problem and sin to our Almighty Father, asking Him to help us through it and explain what we did wrong and what we should do differently.

#6. We must not believe the devil's suggestions or let him stand in the way. Never underestimate Satan's tactics, and be alert for signs of his activity. The Bible promises, "Resist the devil, and he will flee from you. Draw near to God, and he will draw near to you" (James 4:7-8).

Question 5: How can we effectively recognize the devil's voice?

Do people frequently try to get as close to an electric wire as possible without getting shocked? Might you find yourself attempting to get close enough to electricity to just feel a little tickle?

Of course not!

The truth is, treating sin and the devil that way is

even more foolish than doing it with an electric wire. It is Satan who tempts us to get as close to sin as we can, but let's ignore him and instead treat all evil like high voltage.

#7. Fellowship with other Christians provides significant aid in helping us walk the Christian walk. If we have not already, we do well to get in contact with a Christian group that can provide much-needed encouragement and accountability.

#8. We must not compromise our time with God, which includes reading the Bible, praying, singing, meditating about His Word and will, or quietly basking in the holiness of His presence.

If we do not train our desires, emotions, and thoughts to align with truth and integrity, they will align with self-deception. Overcoming temptation requires training, not just willpower. Christianity is not about settling into a comfort zone but rigorously disciplining ourselves to follow Jesus, no matter what.

Below, I have inserted my list of twelve thoughts I try to review frequently and never forget:

1. "Search me, O God, and know my heart: try me, and know my thoughts: And see if there be any wicked way in me, and lead me in the way everlasting" (Psalms 139:23–24).

2. As Christians, we are always clocked in on God's time clock. We are God's private warriors in a raging fight for truth and right. Each time we succumb to temptation we lose a battle for our team.

3. God is ever-present. He knows our thoughts, and we can hide nothing from Him. He is not only watching us, but He is writing everything down.

4. When the devil tempts us, we must promptly rebuke him and seek God's presence.

5. Our body is God's temple, and we must care for and respect it with reverence. "Or do you not know that your body is a temple of the Holy Spirit within you, whom you have from God? You are not your own, for you were bought with a price" (1 Corinthians 6:19-20). (Also 1 Corinthians 3:16-17)

6. "When we want to be something other than the thing God wants us to be, we must be wanting what, in fact, will not make us happy" – C. S. Lewis. [78]

7. When making decisions, ask yourself, "What would Jesus do?" If we would be ashamed to discuss it with God as an action we did or a thought we entertained, then we should not do it.

8. We will always regret ignoring God's will for us.

9. God depends on us to carry out His will; let us not disappoint Him.

10. We should leave our daily schedule in God's hands.

11. God cherishes the time we spend with Him.

12. We must allow nothing to get between us and our Lord.

Study Romans 6-8 for further motivation in over-coming this horrible enemy, and I recommend Louie Giglio's book, Don't Give the Enemy a Seat at Your Table, for further powerful tips on living above sin.

Dead to the world would I be, O Father!
Dead unto sin and alive unto Thee;
Crucify all the earthly within me,
Emptied of sin and self would I be.

I would be Thine and serve Thee forever,
Filled with Thy Spirit, lost in Thy love;
Come to my heart, Lord, come with anointing.
Showers of grace sent down from above.

Open the wells of grace and salvation,
Pour the rich streams deep into my heart;
Cleanse and refine my thought and affection,
Seal me and make me pure as Thou art.[79]
– Elisha A. Hoffman

12. Building a Vibrant Relationship with God

A Christian who does not daily train to follow
and obey the living Jesus is like an athlete who
doesn't train—very ineffective.[80] – Steve Simms

God has not bowed to our nervous haste nor embraced
the methods of our machine age. It is well that we
accept the hard truth now: the man who would know
God must give time to Him![81] – A. W. Tozer

Might we sit still long enough to take in what
God has for us? That is the greatest investment
we will ever make.[82] – Ravi Zacharias

After taking the initial step of surrendering one's life to God, it is essential to build a strong relationship with Him. In fact, God craves to have an intimate bond with us. Christ himself explained the importance of this relationship. He compares himself to a vine and refers to us Christians as the branches coming out of that vine: "I am the vine; you are the branches. Whoever abides in me and I in him, he it is that bears much fruit, for apart from me you can do nothing" (John 15:5).

God is also like a sprinkler system in that those who get close cannot help but obtain His character. He yearns to draw us to Himself so we might become more like Him. Nonetheless, we must choose whether we will let God draw us close.

Becoming like Christ should be the highest goal of every Christian.

What can you do to be more like Jesus? I recommend you make a list of things you can do to be more like our Perfect Example and then do them. Being more like Christ will bring us closer to him, and as we get closer to Christ, he will help us become even more like himself.

Sometimes, we will feel the distance between God and us growing, and we may be tempted to think God is moving away from us. But let us remember, we will always be the ones who moved away. We must have gotten distracted and started taking our focus off God and His will.

* * * * *

I encourage you to read the Holy Bible, especially the New Testament, and live according to the truths you find. Yes, the Bible is large and contains tedious sections and passages that are hard to understand. It will be beneficial to seek God's guidance each time before you read. Ask Him to guide your thoughts so you receive maximum benefit from the words you read.

When reading God's Word, it is also important to take it for what it says instead of what we wish it said or did not say. When folks have not fully yielded themselves to God's instruction, it is easy and convenient to get a wrong idea from the scripture they read.

If you believe a verse means one thing, and Sam is sure it means something else, and I take it still a different way—that is the road to confusion. In such situations, we are twisting the Bible to fit our wills instead of surrendering to it as submissive servants should. Such action has led millions of Christians away from biblical truths.

When we read God's book with diligence and an open mind, we will find the best description of how to live a satisfying life.

> The law of the Lord is perfect, reviving the soul; the testimony of the Lord is sure, making wise the simple; the precepts of the Lord are right, rejoicing the heart; the commandment of the Lord is pure, enlightening the eyes; the fear of the Lord is clean, enduring forever; the rules of the Lord are true, and righteous altogether. More to be desired are they than gold, even much fine gold; sweeter also than honey and drippings of the honey-comb. Moreover, by them is your servant warned; in keeping them there is great reward (Psalms 19:7–11).

* * * * *

Food for the spiritual being—prayer, Bible study, and communication with other Christians—is essential for all Christians, but these have little effect if our minds are set on our own desires. It is when God's will is our utmost focus that communicating with Him can bring miracles.

When Jesus walked the Earth, he was exceptional at helping folks overcome their physical problems. When blind people came to Him requesting sight, they got it. Even today, prayer directly connects us to this same Jesus. Reuben A. Torrey's book *How to Pray* offers excellent insight and instructions on prayer.

If we humbly and openly tell God how we feel when experiencing tough times, He will do a thorough job of consulting and helping us cope with our challenges.

New Christians will often find their current problems to be less of a problem. Yes, the battle will continue to be fierce, but when we maintain a close bond with God, He will be right by our side.

So, take your problems to the Lord and leave them there. Here is the process I use: (I only intend the following prayers to be an example of the mindset we need to have.)

Question 10: Can God help His people find victory over vices such as painful memories, fear, and addictions?

- You may need to renounce Satan by deliberately rejecting his presence and ideas: "Satan, you and your ideas are not welcome here."

Then address God: "Father, you are the solution to all my problems. Be with me as I face life's challenges."

- Surrender to God's will: "Search me, O God, and know my heart. Try me and know my thoughts, and see if there is any wicked way in me and lead me in the way everlasting. Father, I am coming to you in search of truth. Here is my problem; what should I do about it?"

- Then, with God by your side, analyze and think through your problem. God will not always supply the answer directly. But in my experiences, He never fails to guide my thoughts, and I always reach a conclusion with which I can feel at peace.

- Don't forget to thank God: "Thank you, Father. My gratitude is beyond words. I am so unworthy of your attention. Help me not to forget my commitment to Your principles."

When we are tempted to worry or feel overwhelmed with all that needs to be done, we need to again put our life and all its details into God's hands and leave Him have control.

In the years I have been taking my problems to God, He has never let me down. Each time I humbly and submissively pray about an issue, God reassures me that the situation is in His hands and His will is being done. Countless times, the solution to my problem and my best line of action became clear minutes after I prayed about it.

It just happened again: I wrote the first two words in the above sentence, but could not think of a good way to finish the thought. I concluded that I needed God's help to describe God's help, and was thrilled that I was about to experience the help from God that I was trying to describe. After thanking God for His ever-present aid and dependable guidance, I asked Him to help me get this worded properly. Seconds after I finished praying, the rest of the sentence came to my mind.

Exercising Faith in God's Plan

Imagine driving a passenger who keeps telling you to go faster or slower, and when to hit the brakes. But you know the route better than he does, and he just got his driver's license last year, and you were driving for 20 years.

In comparison, how does God feel when we do that to Him? Yes, many times God drives very differently than we would. But God is saying, "My child, trust me. This is what is best for you. You need to go through this so I can teach you something that you can't learn any other way."

We continually need to pursue confidence in God's plan for us. We do best to appreciate who we are and recognize that God needs us exactly as He made us to accomplish His plan.

I am confident we will be the most satisfied when we let God have His way, even when it contradicts how we think. Our weak judgment and narrow view can never compete with God's all-wise guidance.

So, let us put our heavenly Father in the driver's seat of our lives and leave our hands off the controls. If our life is rotten, it is likely because we have control.

I'll share another experience of mine that illustrates the enrichment of life when God is in control: I did much of this writing in the later hours, between 9:00 PM and midnight. I found if I stop writing and go to bed because it is getting late, I will have an attitude at the alarm clock in the morning. In contrast, if I keep writing until my mind slows down, I get to a good stopping place, and I feel obligated to now go to bed, I will wake up feeling marvelous.

This morning is an excellent example. Last night, I worked on this manuscript until 12:20 AM. When I went to bed, I kept thinking about this project, and before long, I got up to take some notes. I got caught up in other aspects of editing, and it was 1:30 before I got to bed again. Now, I am writing this paragraph twenty minutes before I usually get up because I was done sleeping and got out of bed early—which is rare.

Sometimes, God's will looks unreasonable, and we cannot see why He would desire such absurdity. It helps if we think of ourselves as tools in His hands. We must repeatedly say, "Your will be done." Then, we must take a deep breath and do whatever He asks us. Let us endeavor to remember that God's way is always best, even if it looks scary and impossible.

God's plan for us is better in all aspects than our plans for ourselves. I assure you again, friend, that living in and trusting God's will is the only way to find true repose.

Question 11: "How do I know what God's will is for my life?"

Prayer and Our Relationship with God

As "heirs with Christ," we have the potential to influence many of the world's actions and decisions through heartfelt prayer. Apostle James recorded, "The prayer of a righteous person has great power as it is working. Elijah was a man with a nature like ours, and he prayed fervently that it might not rain, and for three years and six months it did not rain on the earth. Then he prayed again, and heaven gave rain, and the earth bore its fruit" (James 5:16–18). Could humanity's current corrupted state be a reality because few dedicate themselves to entreating God for man's regeneration?

A Christian should talk with God throughout the day, similar to how one converses with a friend. In his book, *The Heart of God*, David G. Burkholder shares these encouraging words about building a close relationship with God:

> Do we want a close relationship with the One who will be our "friend that sticketh closer than a brother"? We will find the heart of God first in

His Word. There we see God's heart in His son, Jesus Christ. We learn to know God's heart through the Holy Spirit in our lives. As we open our heart to His heart, He sups with us and we with Him, and we can learn to know Him better and better. This experience is guaranteed to end like the journey of Enoch, who walked with God until the day God took him home. What a glorious prospect![83]

Indeed, we will never regret not compromising our time with God.

But the devil hates when Christians associate with God, and he will attempt to distract us to reduce or delay such action. In fact, when we commit our lives to God, Satan also commits to doing all he can to make us fall.

We must frequently seek a secluded place and, if necessary, silence our devices so we can be alone with God. We will continually fight distractions, but thankfully, Satan has his limits. If we persevere, we shall find that the serenity of being close to God is certainly worth the battle.

If we pray without surrendering our will, we may read things into God's mind, because of our bias, that contradicts what He is trying to tell us. Many people have developed strange ideas, which they felt God was endorsing, when they failed to submit their will in prayer. To effectively locate God's will for us, we must wholly surrender to it, or our desires will mislead us. The book *The Kneeling Christian*, by an unknown Christian, illustrates the importance of sincere prayer. I had one of my most profound encounters with God in a prayer session that was prompted while reading this book.

So, what is keeping you from walking hand in hand with your loving Creator?

＊ ＊ ＊ ＊ ＊

I wish you well as you journey toward a satisfied mind and pursue leaving earthly pleasures ever behind. When you get this accomplished, you will certainly find it was worth every battle on that long upward grind.

I hope to meet you on the other side—with the victories won and the tears all dried.

> Whatever you need,
> The Savior takes heed
> And God answers prayer.
> This promise is true,
> It's written for you,
> If only you dare.
> Do trust in the Lord,
> Depend on His word,
> Believe that He cares.
> He'll show the way out,
> And settle your doubt
> By answering prayer.
>
> When men pray today,

God opens the way
And shows them His will.
He wants us to know,
The right way to go,
His work to fulfill.
Though dark be the night,
He promised the Light
If we would be true.
To heed His sweet voice,
When given a choice
And follow Him through.[84]
– Leon H. Ellis

Oh, how happy are they
Who their Savior obey,
And have laid up their treasures above!
Oh, what tongue can express
The sweet comfort and peace
Of a soul in its earliest love.[85]
– Charles Wesley

The Contentment Dilemma

Further Questions and Their Explanations

Question 1: If God is big enough to create this massive universe, does He care about these tiny humans dwelling on one of the billions of planets He made? Does He really care if we are good or bad?

If your dearest friend were to shrink to the size of a gnat, would you care less about them? Though we are microscopic compared to the rest of the universe, God has every ability to know all about us. He gave special attention to making man and even went as far as making us "in His own image" (Genesis 1:27). Christ's death on the cross is also a powerful indicator of God's love for us.

Yes, God deeply cares about us and our attitude toward right living.

Question 2: What may have been God's motive to give us choice and not just solve many problems, pain, and complications by making us robots?

I believe that making us robots would have missed the whole point of our creation. God wants to connect to humans personally, but you cannot have a personal relationship with a robot. God also wants us to choose to love and honor Him, and this would not have been possible if we could not alternatively choose evil. In *The Case for Faith,* Lee Strobel quotes Peter Kreeft on this subject:

> Then why didn't God create a world without human freedom?
>
> Because that would have been a world without humans. Would it have been a place without hate? Yes. A place without suffering? Yes. But it also would have been a world without love, which is the highest value in the universe. That highest good never could have been experienced. Real love—our love of God and our love of each other—must involve a choice. But with the granting of that choice comes the possibility that people would choose instead to hate.[86]

Question 3: If God and Satan are both in the universe, why is God not contaminated by the devil?

One can mix water into oil, but the water molecules will not mix with the oil. Similarly, as Satan cannot contaminate God, neither does the presence of God cleanse Satan.

Question 4: People from other belief systems associate with their gods and can feel at peace. How can you know your relationship with God is real while theirs is counterfeit?

(Please take the following answer as a suggestion. I cannot guarantee most of the thoughts in this explanation, but they sound logical to my friends and me.)

I am confident all other religions are incorrect, including some belief systems that claim space under the Christian umbrella. Christians lump all supernatural powers together into two categories— God and Satan. Each faith, however, has its preferred names for these deities, and some religions refer to the different characteristics of these deities as individual gods.

Evidence points toward the Holy Bible as the most likely religious book to be true. Thus, I believe and obey the Bible and fall into the Christian category. All views of God and Satan that contradict the Bible are inaccurate, most of the time twisted to fit the agenda of the people who developed them.

If people from other religions associate with a higher power, it must be either God or Satan, but no, their relationship is not necessarily counterfeit.

So, if people from other religions genuinely connect with God, why doesn't God show them the truth about Him?

God will not force the facts on anybody. If these people are not open to the truth, they cannot receive it. On the other hand, if anyone wants to know the truth, God will reveal it to them—that is, if the messenger He calls to present it is willing to do it.

Do people from other religions feel the same

underlying confidence in their stand as Christians do?

I took this question to the One who knows all things, and He assured me the peace and inner assurance Christians enjoy is unique to Christianity. Although folks from other religions may claim complete inner confidence, they have not experienced the Christian's confidence with which to compare it.

To read more on this topic, check out Chapter 5 in Lee Strobel's book, *The Case for Faith*.

Question 5: How can you be sure God speaks to you when thoughts pop into your head? How do you know it is not the devil trying to trick you?

First, let me clarify that there are many times when God is silent, and He wants us to step forward in faith instead of depending on His detailed guidance.

As for thoughts that pop into our heads, we can discover a message's source similar to how we instantly identify our mother's voice. We need to be familiar with our mother's voice to recognize it. Likewise, the more we acquaint ourselves with God, the more readily we identify His messages.

As for the messages I receive potentially being random, I find them much too specific to be unintentional.

I sometimes discern the message's source by the emotions I experience at the time of its arrival. If I feel calm and surprisingly peaceful in my current external environment, it is probably from God. If the message is the wrong style and lacks serenity, it must come from Satan. I also find Satan's messages to be urgent, strongly suggesting to act before thinking. But I admit I do not always know the source of these impressions offhand.

Martin Wells Knapp speaks much about discerning God's voice in *Impressions*. He presents this helpful guide and pointers:

> All impressions which are from above bear the four following distinguishing features. They are:
>
> 1. Scriptural—In harmony with God's will as revealed in His Word.
>
> 2. Right—In harmony with God's will as revealed in man's moral nature.
>
> 3. Providential—In harmony with God's will as revealed in His providential dealings.
>
> 4. Reasonable—In harmony with God's will as revealed to a spiritually enlightened judgment.
>
> Many impressions are so evidently of God that they need no testing, but all that are in any ways doubtful should be summoned before this infallible court of final appeal.
>
> Every impression from above has upon it the Divine Stamp: S. R. P. R.
>
> S-criptural
>
> R-ight

P-rovidential

R-easonable

It is perilous to act on an impression that lacks any of these letters.

… Impressions from above, when followed, are attended by a sweet peace and the consciousness that they are right; those from below, by perplexity and the feeling that something is wrong. The first brings rest; the second robs of it.

… Impressions from below are destitute of spiritual heat. Satan can counterfeit the light of truth but not the ardent glow of holy love. Hence impressions from him bring spiritual chill and discomfort instead of warmth and satisfaction.[87]

On a podcast about spiritual warfare, Rick Rhodes[88] speaks on conviction from God versus accusation from Satan. He illustrates how conviction from God has hope in it and presents the message, "This is what you do to make it right." Whereas accusation from the devil is always a message of despair and hopelessness. The underlying conclusion of Satan's messages is, "You are worthless."

Question 6: You say God knows everything. How can we choose our actions if God already knows the future? Also, if God knew humanity would be so corrupt, why did He create humans in the first place?

Although God knows everything that will happen in the future, He has given us the privilege of choosing what we will do and believe. In our minds, the idea of us having the freedom to choose our actions while God can know the future appears like a contradiction. But are not "God's ways higher than our ways and His thoughts than our thoughts"? (Taken from Isaiah 55:9). Does our inability to comprehend how God functions give us the right to doubt Him?

I think one reason God created humanity, even when He knew it would become exceedingly corrupt, is because He anticipated having a relationship with the few who do commit to His will. At any rate, I am certain we will never, in this life, fully grasp how precious we are to God.

Question 7: Why did God make it so hard for us that no human, besides Christ, can live a sin-free existence?

Who are we to question God's plan? Nonetheless, I thought it might be worth some speculation.

If the best of us could get through life without sinning, would we not try justifying our sins and persuading ourselves that we are sinless? And would we not then be tempted to think we are better than others?

Clearly, God recognized it would be best if it were impossible to have never sinned, which puts all humanity on the same level.

Question 8: (I quote this question and answer from *The Case for Faith* when Lee Strobel asked a question that J. P. Moreland answered.)

"According to Genesis, when God created everything, he declared it was 'good,'" I pointed out. "Obviously, God created hell. But how could he possibly think hell is good? Doesn't that call his character into question?"

"Actually," replies Moreland, "hell was not part of the original creation. Hell is God's fallback position. Hell is something God was forced to make because people chose to rebel against him and turn against what was best for them and the purpose for which they were created.

"You know, when people founded the United States, they didn't start out by creating jails. They would have much rather had a society without jails. But they were forced to create them because people would not cooperate. The same is true for hell."[89]

Question 9: What about the people who live virtuous lives but do not identify with Christianity? Will they go to hell just because they were not Christians?

Following is an excerpt of some more

conversation from Strobel's *The Case for Faith* that addresses this question:

> (Strobel) "But as you conceded, it is important how people live," I say. "People say Gandhi lived a more virtuous life than most Christians. Why should he be sent to hell just because he wasn't a follower of Jesus?"
>
> (Zacharias) "First and foremost, it's important to know that no human being consigns anybody to heaven or hell. In fact, God himself does not send anybody to heaven or to hell; the person chooses to respond to the grace of God or to reject the grace of God, although even that decision is enabled by His grace.
>
> "Second, Abraham asked God in the case of Sodom and Gomorrah whether he was going to let the righteous die with the unrighteous, and it was wonderful how Abraham answered his own question. He says, 'Will not the Judge of all the earth do right?' This means we can be absolutely confident that whatever God does in the case of Gandhi or any other person, He will do what is right" (Emphasis added).[90]

Question 10: Can God help His people overcome vices and distresses such as painful memories, fear, and addictions?

Yes. As His children, Christians will find that God does an excellent job of relieving pain and comforting the soul. He will help His people rise above any obsession if they realize their weakness and surrender their spirit to receiving His divine aid and guidance. "The angel of the Lord encamps around those who fear him, and delivers them" (Psalms 34:7).

The new birth is an excellent example of how God dramatically changes people.

Question 11: How do I know God's will for my life?

If we diligently seek God's will with an open mind and maintain a close relationship with Him, He will reveal it to us. However, I have learned that God sometimes would rather not show me what He has in mind for me in the future. When I insist on knowing God's will for me ahead of time, His response is something to the extent of, "I love you. But I will not share my will before it is my will for you to know it." Nevertheless, in my experiences, God reassured me that His will was being done.

At other times, God might tell us His will because we insist on knowing, even though He may prefer withholding the answer from us at that time. This may be one reason Jesus teaches us to pray with the attitude of "Your will be done."

For the most part, God desires that we think

through the situation and do what we decide is best while trusting Him to guide our conclusion.

Author's Note

Following is a brief outline of my journey in writing this book.

I was thirteen when I made the life commitment to Christianity. A few years later, I started this manuscript as an article, in an effort to help others find the unspeakable contentment I experienced when I surrendered my life to the Lord. Over the next eighteen years and between the productions of various writing projects, this manuscript underwent many expansions and revisions.

Give God the praise if this book has been of any help to you. Of myself, I could have done nothing.

Below is a list of more books I recommend reading as you grow in your Christian life. As with any literature of this type, I recommend seeking God's guidance each time before you start reading so that you may discern between truth and error.

- Doing What Comes Spiritually, by John M. Drescher
- Searching for Meaning, by Lester Bauman (This is a study of Ecclesiastes.)
- Secrets of the Kingdom Life, by David Bercot
- The Heart of God, by David G. Burkholder
- The Kneeling Christian, by an unknown Christian

The Contentment Dilemma

URGENT PLEA!

Thank you for reading this book!
I really appreciate feedback.
I need your input to help make the next edition
of this book and my future books better.

Please take a few minutes to leave an honest review on
Amazon, letting me know what you think of the book:
https://marcushurstauthor.com/review
Thank you.
– Marcus Hurst

Be the first to know when Marcus Hurst's next book is available.
Follow him at https://www.bookbub.com/authors/marcus-hurst
to get an alert whenever he has a new release, discount, or preorder.

The Contentment Dilemma

Bibliography

[1] This quote's origin is unknown.

[2] This quote's origin is unknown.

[3] This was included in an email Ivan sent me on July 14th 2023.

[4] John Esh, *O Praise the Lord* (# 23). Amos Esh. 2010 (Copywrite © 2010 by Amos Esh)

[5] This quote is widely attributed to Friedrich Nietzsche, but there is no concrete evidence that he actually wrote or said it in this exact form. Some sources suggest it might be a paraphrase or misattribution, as it doesn't appear in his known works, though he did write much on the topic.

[6] Abdu Murray, *Saving Truth* (p. 17). Zondervan, 2018

[7] It is not known where this quote was said.

[8] Blaise Pascal, *Pensées (Thoughts).* Digireads.com Publishing, 2018 (ed. 1910)

[9] Dr. Jonathan Swift, *Miscellanies. The Tenth Volume*, (ed. 1745)

[10] Os Guinness, *Time for Truth*, (pp. 79–80). Grand Rapids: Baker. 2000

[11] https://hopethoughts.com/2022/06/30/desire-doesnt-require-obedience/

[12] C. S. Lewis. *Mere Christianity,* (p. 66). HarperOne, 2009 (First published in 1952.)

[13] Charles Caleb Colton, *Lacon.* Hardpress, 2018

---

[14]	https://www.who.int/news/item/12-07-2021-un-report-pandemic-year-marked-by-spike-in-world-hunger
[15]	https://www.who.int/docs/default-source/documents/child-maltreatment/global-status-report-on-violence-against-children-2020/who-gsrpvac-2020-magnitude-consequences-infographic-en.pdf
[16] https://www.who.int/news/item/09-03-2021-devastatingly-pervasive-1-in-3-women-globally-experience-violence
[17]	https://www.who.int/news-room/fact-sheets/detail/abortion
[18]	https://www.who.int/news/item/29-11-2022-who-urges-more-effective-prevention-of-injuries-and-violence--causing-1-in-12-deaths-worldwide/
[19]	https://www.who.int/news-room/fact-sheets/detail/opioid-overdose
[20]	https://www.who.int/news-room/fact-sheets/detail/alcohol
[21] https://btlfamilylaw.com/divorce-statistics/
[22]	https://www.who.int/news-room/fact-sheets/detail/tobacco
[23] https://ourworldindata.org/suicide
[24]	https://www.who.int/news-room/fact-sheets/detail/sexually-transmitted-infections-(stis)
[25]https://www.who.int/data/gho/data/indicators/indicator-details/GHO/number-of-deaths-due-to-hiv-aids
[26] Abdu Murray, *Saving Truth,* (p. 23). Zondervan, 2018
[27]	https://hopethoughts.com/2023/01/05/hey-there-heightened-awareness-is-calling/#like-34548
[28] https://hopethoughts.com/2022/04/11/an-appeal-to-free-will-is-often-a-false-flag
[29]	https://hopethoughts.com/2022/11/16/is-self-love-a-

pleasurable-path/

[30] John Esh, *O Praise the Lord* (# 23). Amos Esh. 2010 (Copywrite © 2010 by Amos Esh)

[31] Lee Strobel, *The Case for Faith,* (p. 252 & 255). Zondervan, 2000

[32] B. E. Warren, *Christian Endeavor Songs #2* (# 168). Prairie View Press, 1986

[33] Os Guinness, *God in the Dark,* (pp. 65-66). Crossway, 1996

[34] Hank Hanegraaff, *Truth Matters, Life Matters More,* (p. 15). Thomas Nelson, 2019

[35] F. F. Bruce, The New Testament Documents: Are They Reliable? Eerdmans, 2003

[36] Lee Strobel, *The Case for Faith,* (p. 150). Zondervan, 2000

[37] Merrill F, Unger, *The New Unger's Bible Dictionary.* The Moody Bible Institute of Chicago, 1988 (First published in 1957.)

[38] Os Guinness, *God in the Dark,* (p. 12). Crossway, 1996.

[39] Isaac Watts, *Zion's Praises* (# 50). Weaver Music Company, 1987.

[40] Os Guinness, God in the Dark, (pp. 166-167). Crossway, 1996.

[41] Lee Strobel, *The Case for Faith,* (p. 38). Zondervan, 2000.

[42] C. S. Lewis, *The Problem of Pain,* (p. 31). HarperOne, 2009 (First published in 1940.)

[43] A. W. Tozer, *The Pursuit of God,* (p. 74). Grapevine, 2022 (First published in 1948.)

[44] Patrick Morley, *How God Makes Men,* (p. 167). Multnomah Books, 2013

[45] Lee Rufener, *The Heartbeat of the Remnant—Summer 2022,* (pp. 16-17). Berean Voice, 2022

[46] Lee Strobel, *The Case for Faith,* (p. 50). Zondervan, 2000

[47] Leon Horning, Besides the Still Waters devotional series

---

(February 14th, 2020)

[48] Patrick Morley, *How God Makes Men,* (p. 132). Multnomah Books, 2013

[49] "K" in Rippon's Selection of Hymns, 1787, *Mennonite Hymns* (# 171). Weaverland Conference Mennonite congregations, 2015

[50] Baddie Mason & Eddie Carswell, *O Praise the Lord* (# 88). 2010 (Copywrite © 1993 Dayspring Music, LLC)

[51] This quote's origin is unknown.

[52] C. S. Lewis, *Mere Christianity,* (pp. 123-124). HarperOne, 2009 (First published in 1952.)

[53] Joanna Gaines, The World Needs Who You Where Made to Be. Thomas Nelson, 2020

[54] David G. Burkholder, *The Heart of God.* Eastern Mennonite Publications, 2009

[55] Martin Wells Knapp, *Impressions,* (Ch. 2). Jawbone Digital, 2017 (First published in 1892.)

[56] David G. Burkholder, The Heart of God, (p. 159). Eastern Mennonite Publications, 2009

[57] John Esh, *O Praise the Lord,* (# 38). Amos Esh. 2010 (Copywrite © 2010 by Amos Esh)

[58] Ravi Zacharias, *The Logic of God,* (p. 237). Zondervan, 2019

[59] C. S. Lewis, *Mere Christianity,* (p. 179). HarperOne, 2009

[60] Lee Strobel, *The Case for Faith* (pp. 51–52). Zondervan, 2000

[61] Norman Troyer mentioned this in a personal correspondence.

[62] Abdu Murray, *Saving Truth,* (p. 23). Zondervan, 2018

[63] Clarence E. Jones, *I Stand before Him Guilty.* James D. Vaughan Music Publisher

[64] C. S. Lewis, *The Great Divorce,* (p. 68). HarperCollins, 1973 (First published in 1946.)

[65] Lee Strobel, *The Case for Faith,* (pp. 174–175). Zondervan,

2000

[66] C. S. Lewis, *The Great Divorce,* (p. 68). HarperCollins, 1973 (First published in 1946.)

[67] Eden R. Latta, *Christian Hymnal* (# 292)

[68] A. W. Tozer, *The Pursuit of God.* (p. 75). Grapevine, 2022 (First published in 1948.)

[69] https://hopethoughts.com/2022/04/11/an-appeal-to-free-will-is-often-a-false-flag

[70] Dr. Dennis Swanberg & Ron Smith, *The Man Code* (p.16). Worthy Publishers, 2009

[71] A. W. Tozer, The Pursuit of God. (p. 78). Grapevine, 2022 (First published in 1948.)

[72] Ravi Zacharias, The Logic of God, (p. 280). Zondervan, 2019

[73] C. S. Lewis, *Mere Christianity,* (p. 29). HarperOne, 2009 (First published in 1952.)

[74] Calvin Horst, *Is My Treasure in Heaven*, Unpublished as of Nov. 2024

[75] It is not known where this quote was said.

[76] David W. Hegg, The Obedience Option: Because God Knows What's Good for Us, 2010

[77] Reuben A. Torrey, Edward D. Andrews, *How to Succeed in the Christian Life [Updated and Expanded]*, Christian Publishing House, 2016

[78] C. S. Lewis, *The Problem of Pain,* (p. 31). HarperOne, 2009 (First published in 1940.)

[79] Elisha A. Hoffman, *Christian Hymnal* (#371). Gospel Publishers, 1959

[80] https://hopethoughts.com/2022/09/09/christians-should-train-like-navy-seals-so-they-can-follow-jesus-better/

[81] A. W. Tozer, *God's Pursuit of Man*, (p. 10). Grapevine, 2022

(First published in 1950.)

[82] Ravi Zacharias, *The Logic of God,* (p. 42). Zondervan, 2019

[83] David G. Burkholder, *The Heart of God,* (pp. 57-58). Eastern Mennonite Publications, 2009

[84] Leon H. Ellis, *Christian Endeavor Songs #3* (# 157). Prairie View Press, 2001

[85] Charles Wesley, *Mennonite Hymns* (# 234). Weaverland Conference Mennonite congregations, 2015

[86] Lee Strobel, *The Case for Faith,* (pp. 37–38). Zondervan, 2000

[87] Martin Wells Knapp, *Impressions,* (Ch. 5). Jawbone Digital, 2017 (First published in 1892.)

[88] https://www.asherwitmer.com/rick-rhodes-on-christians-and-spiritual-warfare/

[89] Lee Strobel, *The Case for Faith,* (p. 175). Zondervan, 2000

[90] Lee Strobel, *The Case for Faith,* (p. 157). Zondervan, 2000

www.ingramcontent.com/pod-product-compliance
Lightning Source LLC
Chambersburg PA
CBHW051729040426
42447CB00008B/1044